OCCASIONAL ADDRESSES

OCCASIONAL ADDRESSES

1893–1916

BY THE

RIGHT HON. HERBERT HENRY ASQUITH
1st Earl of Oxford and Asquith

Essay Index Reprint Series

BOOKS FOR LIBRARIES PRESS
FREEPORT, NEW YORK

First Published 1918
Reprinted 1969

STANDARD BOOK NUMBER:
8369-1368-X

LIBRARY OF CONGRESS CATALOG CARD NUMBER:
76-99715

PRINTED IN THE UNITED STATES OF AMERICA

M. A.

LABORVM GAVDIORVM LVCTVVM

CONSORTI

D.D.

H. H. A.

PREFACE

THE Addresses collected in this volume have been delivered on various occasions during the last twenty-five years. They deal with diverse subjects, and have only a negative connection with one another: none of them trenches upon the domain of controversial politics. Though by nature (as I believe) of a pacific temperament, I have been constrained by the force of circumstances to divide nearly the whole of my active life between two of the most contentious of professions. A man who spends most of his days and nights in the Law Courts and the House of Commons has a special need for the soothing and cleansing influences of literature and scholarship. His time for reading, still more for research, is of necessity limited; but there is nothing, even in the absorbing demands of a dual vocation, that requires him to abate his interest either in the ancient masterpieces or in the newest phases of the Arts. And if he takes advantage of such opportunities as present themselves from time to time to put forward opinions and judgments upon literary and academic themes, his critics will in justice remember— what he is not likely himself to forget—that such productions are from the nature of the case the work, not of an expert, but of an amateur.

I have added some appreciations of the lives and characters of distinguished men whose deaths have been the occasion of public sorrow.

In the compilation and revision of the volume I have been more indebted than I can say to the wise counsels and helping hand of my old friend, Mr. Edmund Gosse.

H. H. A.

January 1918.

CONTENTS

OCCASIONAL ADDRESSES

I

CRITICISM

I

CRITICISM [1]

THE subject upon which I am about to offer you
a few observations is one which I have selected
because it has always appeared to me that, if
what is called " the higher education " is worthy
of the name, it ought to stimulate and guide the
power and practice of criticism in its best and
largest sense. I cannot profess to treat the
matter in the exhaustive and scientific fashion
which it deserves. What I have to say has been
hastily put together under the storm and stress
of pressing occupations, and if you find, as I
fear you will, that it is at the same time desultory
and dogmatic, I must ask you to be indulgent to
one who has got out of the practice of lecturing.

What do we mean by Criticism ? What are
its functions and its limits ? These are the
questions which I propose briefly to discuss.
Let us upon the threshold disabuse our minds of
one or two misleading and narrowing associations

[1] Delivered to the students of the London Society for the
Extension of University Teaching, April 23, 1898.

which have gathered round the term Criticism in popular thought and speech. In the eyes of a great number of people a critic is nothing more than a censor, a critical attitude is equivalent to an attitude of disparagement, and criticism is only another name for the science of finding fault. According to the famous gibe of Lord Beaconsfield, himself a great man of letters and a great man of action, who in both characters had had more than his share of ungenerous treatment from the commentators of the day, " the critics are the men who have failed in literature and in art." Whether the phrase is his own, or, as we are told, borrowed from Landor or from Balzac, it expresses a view of the professors of criticism which is neither uncommon nor unnatural in those who are their favourite targets. It is of course true that there have been eminent men in whom their own want of success in the sphere of action or production has at once stimulated and soured the critical faculty. But it is not in this dwarfed and distorted sense that we are using the term to-day. Denigration, whether it springs from baffled rivalry, or from a morose and cynical temper, or from honest shortsightedness, often amuses, is sometimes useful, may now and then—in the hands of a writer like Junius—exhibit some of the highest qualities of literary art ; but it is not criticism.

There is another and a more legitimate applica-

tion of the word which nevertheless requires to
be closely watched. No antithesis is commoner
than that between criticism and construction.
We say of writers, of literatures, of epochs, that
one is constructive and another critical, as
though the faculties of creation and judgment
could not be brought to their highest perfection
in the same mental climate and environment.
Such a theory squares very ill both with the
psychology of intellectual production, and with
the facts recorded in the history of literature and
art. It is true that there are unique outbursts of
creative genius which baffle the analysis and defy
the so-called laws of the philosophical historian.
The wind blows where and when it lists, and no
formula of heredity or of adaptation will account
for the appearance at a particular time and place
of a Dante or a Shakespeare. But the most
conspicuous eras of intellectual fecundity—the
ages of Pericles and Augustus, of Elizabeth and
Louis XIV., of the *Sturm und Drang*, of Scott
and Byron—have produced not only great poets
and great historians, but great critics also. It is
not even true that in the intellectual world itself
the division of labour has ever been carried to
such a point that one set of men produce works
of art, while another set theorise about its principles and formulate its canons. Look at Plato,
Bacon, Goethe—to take only names which stand
in the front rank—and ask yourselves how much

of their work, if it came to be analysed, would be found to be creative and how much critical. A great artist may be incapable of criticism, and a good critic may be incapable of creation. But neither in the individual nor in the generations of men does the one set of gifts exclude the other. Criticism in the true sense has a positive as well as a negative function. By discriminating between that which is true and that which is false, between good and bad art, between reality and imposture, by dethroning the ephemeral idols of fashion, and recalling the wandering crowd to the worship of beauty and of greatness, criticism plays the part of a vitalising and energising force in social and intellectual progress. It performs the double duty of solvent and stimulant. To take a single example, it was the essentially critical speculations of Hume which, as we know from their own avowal, awoke Kant from his " dogmatic slumber," and first " caused the scales to fall from the eyes " of Bentham, and thereby became, at any rate, the indirect occasion for two rival schemes of constructive philosophy. There is no emptier fallacy than to suppose that criticism is merely a form of intellectual gymnastic—the appropriate pastime of epochs of torpor and stagnation—the business of second-rate minds in the relatively barren intervals which separate the great vintage years in the history of human culture. The business of criticism, as Matthew Arnold says in a well-known passage, is " to know the best that is known and thought in the world, and by in its turn making this known to create a current of true and fresh ideas."

Nor, again, ought we entirely to confine our attention to the perfectly legitimate, but at the same time the narrow and technical, sense in which criticism is understood to describe the processes by which specific rules of interpretation and canons of taste are developed and formulated Like every other form of intellectual activity, it may be specialised within the confines of a definite subject matter, as it is, for instance, in the textual criticism of literature, and in the aesthetic criticism of the arts. Both have at various times fascinated the interest and absorbed the energies of some of the best intellects of the race. Few things indeed in literary history are more striking than the effect produced by the sudden unsealing of the treasure-houses of class-ical antiquity in the middle of the fifteenth century. The critical activity of Europe, which had been for generations frittering itself away upon the barren analyses of scholasticism, found in the study and collation of the ancient texts an untried field of boundless extent and inexhaust-ible fertility. The Stephenses, the Scaligers, the Casaubons, were but the most conspicuous figures in a huge army of enthusiastic, even fanatical,

explorers—the confessors and martyrs of a new
literary faith, of which the humbler rank and file
have been depicted ﹙for us with incomparable
fidelity and pathos in Browning's *Grammarian's
Funeral*. Their work has been continued from
that time to this by an unbroken chain of successors, to which we here in England, with our
Bentley and our Porson, may claim to have
contributed some of the highest names. The
science of textual criticism is constantly annexing
new territories and developing wider and more
penetrating methods ; and in its application to
sacred literature, and to the slowly deciphered
records of the great religions and civilisations of
the East, it has achieved in our own time some
of its most memorable results.

If we turn to the other example, which I
mentioned a moment ago, of the more specialised
fields of critical activity—the aesthetic criticism
of the arts—it will, I think, be found that the
output, though even more copious, possesses in
a far lower degree the qualities either of scientific
exactitude or of practical utility. The plain
man, who seeks salvation with the art critics,
very soon finds that he has condemned himself
to wander in a blind and baffling twilight of
cloudy dogma and chaotic precept. It is true
that aesthetic criticism has been the subject of
some of the greatest masterpieces in literature.
The reading of Lessing's *Laocoon* has been to

many smaller people what it was to Macaulay—
an intellectual revelation. His masterly analysis
of the respective functions on the one side of
painting and the plastic arts, and on the other
of poetry, as the vehicles and organs of aesthetic
representation ; the one employing " forms and
colours in space," the other " articulate sounds
in time " ; and his luminous and precise development of the limitations which those conditions
impose, as regards both subject and treatment,
upon the artist and the poet, have received no
substantial modification or addition from later
thinkers. Nor, again, can any educated Englishman or Englishwoman of our own time forget
the debt of enjoyment and suggestion which he
or she owes to the intellectual independence, the
spiritual insight, the golden-tongued eloquence,
of John Ruskin. But as a rule it must, I think,
be said of art criticism that it has a blighting
effect even upon good writers; that it has been
comparatively unproductive either in speculative
or in practical guidance; and that it consists to
a large extent in the unilluminating discussion of
unreal problems in unintelligible language. Horn
said of Goethe that everywhere in him " you are
on firm land or island—nowhere the infinite sea."
It is exactly the reverse with the bulk of our
modern professors of aesthetic. To change the
metaphor, and to borrow a phrase—I think—
from Matthew Arnold, they seem to spend their

lives in "always beating the bush and never starting the hare." We look in vain for guiding principles in a jungle of jargon. Carlyle tells us that at one time John Sterling took to art criticism, for which he was well fitted by technical and historical knowledge. But, says his biographer, " of all subjects this was the one I cared least to hear even Sterling talk of " ; " indeed," he adds—and I am disposed respectfully to agree with him—" it is a subject on which earnest men, abhorrent of hypocrisy and speech that has no meaning, are admonished to silence in this sad time, and had better . . . perambulate their picture galleries with little or no speech."

But criticism, as I have said, is to be understood in a larger sense than is covered by any of its merely technical applications. It may, I suppose, be roughly defined as the science or art —whichever it is to be called—of passing judgments upon the productions and the acts of men. I say purposely of " passing " and not merely of " forming " judgments, because it seems to be of the essence of criticism that it should be articulate. No one would be foolish enough to set up as a test of the due development of the critical faculty the capacity to compose an essay or to write a review. Some of the best critics whom many of us have known have never made themselves answerable for a line of printed matter. But criticism, as the developed activity of an educated mind, .s clearly something different from the instinctive and unformulated opinions and tastes which the mass of men hold as unconsciously as they " talk prose." To use Hazlitt's admirable phrase, " they think by proxy and talk by rote." Before a man can criticise the works or the doings of his fellows to any purpose, he must have passed beyond this stage. He must have acquired the faculty of seeing things at first hand and for himself, of finding his way to their central meaning, of bringing to bear upon what is new the gathered and reasoned knowledge which he has gained elsewhere, and of expressing in words, intelligible to himself and to others, degrees of comparison and shades of difference. If representation is the function of art, interpretation is the function of criticism.

I am not going to-day to deal with the matter on its historical side. To those who are interested in that aspect of it, I venture to commend the learned and suggestive work of Mr. Worsfold, *The Principles of Criticism*, which has recently been published. But I invite you to consider with me for a few moments what are some of the conditions to which criticism, if it is to be a trustworthy and fruitful organ of interpretation, must conform. The first and perhaps the most obvious requirement of criticism is that it should be open-minded, many-sided, not sectarian but catholic. Partisanship, which in the active conduct of human affairs is an almost indispensable motive power, is fatal to the wholesome exercise of the critical faculty. " It is the part of a man like you," wrote Voltaire to Vauvenargues, " to have preferences, but no exclusions." The moment the critic becomes the disciple, or still worse the propagandist, of a school—the moment he assumes the prophetic mantle, and begins to deal in sentences of excommunication and threats of anathema—he abdicates his proper function, which is that not of a preacher but of an interpreter. With many great authors—Carlyle and Ruskin are famous examples—criticism becomes a mere vehicle for the trenchant and fervid exposition of a creed in which the writer himself has a vivid faith, and for the defence of which he often finds his most effective plan of campaign to consist in bringing out and driving home the fallacies and shortcomings of rival systems. This may be and often is a work of the highest literary and social value, but to carry it on with vigour and success requires the temper of the controversialist or the missionary, not the temper of the critic. One may perhaps be permitted to suggest even of so finished a master of the art as Matthew Arnold that his growing zeal against Philistines, dissenters, and dogmatists, if it did not actually blur the clear serenity of his vision, at any rate in time diminished both the quantity and the value of his contributions to criticism. May we not add that it is a sure sign of the degeneration of the critic, as such, when he lapses into the habitual use of catch-words and formulae ? There is nothing more hampering to the free and elastic play of the judgment than the habit, easily acquired because it saves trouble, of drawing one's words and phrases from a particular literary or artistic dialect.

Another distinguishing mark of criticism in its best and largest sense is that it should be impersonal. This criterion does not in the least imply that it should be uncoloured by the personality of the critic, or that it should ignore the personal element in the antecedents, the structure, or the style of the work upon which judgment is pronounced. What it means is this—that criticism ought to aim at a disinterested appreciation of whatever is worthy or unworthy in its subject matter, and should not be merely or mainly a pretext for the display of the resources of the critic. The importance of this particular precept can be best illustrated by one or two examples of the mischief which results from its neglect. Take for instance the methods of the founders of the *Edinburgh Review.* With all their occasional dexterity and their conspicuous freshness and force, they perpetually suggest that the governing purpose of the critic is to detect mistakes, to expose absurdities and contradictions—if possible to tear the author to tatters ; but in any case and above all to leave in the mind of the reader an abiding impression of relentless smartness and omniscient facility. In nine cases out of ten the apparent object is to show the skill with which an accomplished executioner can ply the instruments of his calling. Flagellation in the sphere of criticism is often not only a salutary discipline, but a duty of imperative obligation ; and no one but a puling sentimentalist will deny that in the armoury of a well-equipped critic room must be found for the bastinado and even for the knout. But treatment of this kind should be reserved for impenitent dullards and professional impostors—the recidivists of the literary and artistic world. More than two generations of amused and admiring readers have been struck with a sense of painful incongruity in the spectacle of Macaulay bringing into play the whole battery of his well-furnished torture-chamber to rack an ephemeral driveller like Robert Montgomery. Another illustration, in a widely differing style, of the havoc which is wrought in the best-informed criticism by the importunate egotism of the critic is to be found in the writings of one of the greatest masters of style in the whole range of English literature—Thomas de Quincey. From the time of Milton, with perhaps the exception of Burke, it may be doubted whether that unsurpassed instrument of expression—

English prose—has ever been handled with such a width of range, such an easy command of its multitudinous resources, such wealth of imagery, such " flexibility of adaptation," such intuitive apprehension of the subtle laws which define the boundary line between ambition and audacity. A tired man, who goes home after a day of strenuous labour amid the *fumum et opes strepitumque Romae,* can take down from his shelves any one of the fourteen volumes of Professor Masson's admirable edition of De Quincey's works, with the assured certainty that, wherever he opens the book, he will be able to browse for half an hour on rare and succulent pasturage. De Quincey was no doubt more than a critic ; he was an artist of high rank in what he himself calls " the domain of impassioned prose." But, all the same, a large part of his work is critical, and it is vitiated by exactly the defect which I am attempting to describe. I lay no stress upon his incurable and often intolerable prolixity, which sometimes calls to mind the caustic comment of the Scotch judge upon a long-winded advocate—that he " exhausted time and encroached upon eternity." But De Quincey, with all his powers, has in him more than a little of the literary coxcomb. Whatever may be the work or the author that for the time being occupies his pen, he never ceases to be self-conscious ; he rarely fails to remind the reader of his own experiences, tastes, eruditions, accomplishments; and, whether he praises or blames, admires or disparages, you never feel that he has lost himself in his subject, but always that he wishes to interest you in the subject because it interests himself.

I have said that criticism should be catholic and impersonal. Let me add that for its proper exercise it peculiarly needs imagination. The failures of even accomplished critics to interpret the phenomena with which they set themselves to deal are for the most part to be put down, not to dulness—of which they were incapable—nor to prejudice—against which they were sedulously on their guard—but to lack of imaginative insight. It is this defect which has kept whole generations of critics in bondage to the " letter which kills." Literary history is full of examples of this sterilising subservience. The " dramatic unities," the so-called " dignity of history," the conventions by which poetry has been from time to time confined to particular conditions of subject, structure, and measure, are well-known instances. The activity of the imagination is needed to correct this mechanical view, which treats it, to use an excellent comparison of Mr. Saintsbury's, as though it were to be played like a game of whist. The fatal consequences of defective imagination are, of course, nowhere better illustrated than in the criticisms of posterity upon historical characters and events. Mr. Morley, in his study of Voltaire, speaks of the " crippling of his historic imagination," and of the " inability which this inflicted upon him of conceiving the true meaning and lowest roots of the Catholic legend." " The middle age," he goes on, " between himself and the polytheism of the Empire was a parched desert to him and to all his school, just as to the Protestant the interval between the Apostles and Luther is a long night of unclean things." The greatest of English historians, Gibbon himself, is not exempt from the same reproach. When the account comes to be taken between the eighteenth and the nineteenth centuries, it will probably turn out that some of our most vaunted assets are after all bad debts ; but, whatever comes or goes, one can hardly doubt that the establishment which our age has witnessed of the sovereignty of the historic method will be counted to us a clear gain. Whether you are judging a book, a picture, a character, or a movement, no one now dreams of denying that it is the first duty of the critic to put himself, so far as may be, imaginatively at the point of view of his subject, to take into account the antecedents which led up to and the atmosphere which surrounded its production, and not to be a party to that worst form of *ex post facto* legislation which imports modern standards of thought and taste into our judgments of the past.

C

It is perhaps encouraging in this connection to remind ourselves, who are novices in this great art, of the evidence which shows that neither culture, nor intuition, nor the completest union of both, has saved even men of genius from mistakes over which the most humbly equipped student may now make merry. The blunders of great critics would be a fascinating subject in the hands of Mr. Leslie Stephen or Mr. Birrell. This is not the occasion, even if I had the ability, to attempt an exhaustive treatment of it; but I will venture to recall to your memory, from quite modern times, a few conspicuous and familiar instances. Voltaire, who, unlike his literary associate, Frederick the Great, had a real admiration for the genius of Shakespeare, spoke of *Hamlet* as a " rude and barbarous piece—such a work as one might suppose to be the fruit of the imagination of a drunken savage." Dr. Johnson, as you know, emptied the vials of his contempt upon *Lycidas* : " The diction is harsh, the rhymes uncertain, and the numbers unpleasing. . . . Its form is that of a pastoral; easy, vulgar, and therefore disgusting. . . . Among the flocks, and copses, and flowers, appear the heathen deities ; Jove and Phoebus, Neptune and Aeolus, with a long train of mythological imagery, such as a college easily supplies. . . . He who thus grieves will excite no sympathy ; he who thus praises will confer no honour." Not only Johnson, but

Richardson and Goldsmith, failed to see any merit in *Tristram Shandy,* or to detect the zigzag streak of genius in " the man Sterne." " Nothing odd," said the great Doctor, "will do long. *Tristram Shandy* did not last." By the way, I may remind you that of Sterne's Sermons the same potent authority said, perhaps with more reason : "I did read them, but it was in a stage-coach ; I should not have deigned to look at them had I been at large." The great Goethe, to whom if to any one we should look for catholicity of appreciation, told an Italian who asked him his opinion of Dante that he thought " the *Inferno* abominable, the *Purgatorio* dubious, and the *Paradiso* tiresome." This may take us back again for a moment to Voltaire, who himself spoke of Dante as a poet " qu'on loue toujours parce qu'on ne lit guère." Walter Scott, in 1810, when he had just finished *The Lady of the Lake—The Lay of the Last Minstrel* and *Marmion* having already established his poetical reputation—said to James Ballantyne : " If you wish to speak of a real poet, Joanna Baillie is now the highest genius of our country." He added that he had more pleasure in reading Johnson's *London* and *The Vanity of Human Wishes* than any other poetical compositions he could mention. Jeffrey, whose critical reputation is perhaps nowadays quoted rather too low, published in 1828—and, as Mr. Leslie Stephen has shown, was content to leave unretracted and unqualified to the end of his life—this truly astounding judgment on the poetry of his time : " Keats, Shelley, and Wordsworth are melting fast from the fields of vision " ; and the only two contemporary poets in whom he saw any " promise of immortality " he declared to be Rogers and Campbell. That this is not the mere eccentricity of a prosaic *Edinburgh* reviewer, born of caprice or paradox, is proved by the contemporary judgment of no less an authority than Byron himself. In a pamphlet written in 1820, not published in his lifetime, but set out almost at length in Moore's biography, the most popular poet of his age gives his view as to the then state of English poetry. Recollect that he was writing at a time when not only himself and Scott, but Wordsworth, Shelley, and Coleridge had produced their greatest works, and when Keats, whose *Endymion* had been damned two years before in the *Quarterly*, had just brought out the volume which contains *Hyperion, Isabella, Lamia*, and *The Eve of St. Agnes.* What is the judgment of Byron ? " That this is the age of the decline of English poetry," he writes, " will be doubted by few who have calmly considered the subject." Crabbe, he says, is " the first of living poets." And again : " As I told Moore not very long ago, we are all wrong except Rogers, Crabbe, and Campbell." " There will be found," he adds characteristically, " as com-

fortable metaphysics, and ten times more pure
poetry, in Pope's *Essay on Man* than in *The
Excursion.*" Such a strange failure of critical
insight is but poorly redeemed by his subsequent
grudging tribute to the genius of Keats, of whom
he says a year later that, " *malgré* all the fantastic fopperies of his style, he was undoubtedly
of great promise." Take again, as a notable
instance of blurred and distorted vision in a case
where we should have looked for the light and
warmth of vivid sympathy, Carlyle's famous
review of Lockhart's *Life of Scott.* " It seems to
us," he says in a burst of the most challenging
Carlylese, " that there goes other stuff to the
making of great men than can be detected here.
One knows not what idea worthy of the name of
great, what purpose, instinct, or tendency that
could be called great, Scott ever was inspired
with. . . . The great fact [about the Waverley
Novels] is ·that they were faster written and
better paid for than any other books in the
world." They are " addressed to the everyday
mind " ; they are " not profitable for doctrine,
for reproof, or for edification " ; they were not
dragged into being and hammered into shape
with the convulsive throes and at the fuliginous
smithy of genius, but tranquilly " manufactured
with a fatal productive facility." They opened
the floodgates to a " Noah's deluge of ditchwater."
Such is the sentence passed by the greatest of

his countrymen since born upon Scott, because, like Goethe as we know him, and like Shakespeare as we imagine him, he brought forth his master-pieces with the serene detachment, the uncalcu-lating profusion, the majestic effortlessness, which belong only to supreme genius.

These illustrations will suffice. If time per-mitted I might easily add to the catalogue. But any one who presumes to speak even in the most unambitious way about criticism may fairly be asked if there are any practical rules by the observance of which the critical faculty may be trained and enriched. There is great danger in attempting to prescribe such a code. One may be warned by the example of an eminent Scotch writer, who more than a hundred years ago wrote a bulky work, now never read, on the " Elements of Criticism," which elicited from Gold-smith the disagreeable pleasantry that " it was easier to write that book than to read it." Such advice as I would venture to give would be confined to a couple of seeming commonplaces which appear to me to sum up all that can be wisely said upon the matter, and that is, first, to study great models, and secondly, to practise diligently for yourself. As regards the first, excellent and admirable as is the quality of French criticism, there is no need to go beyond our own literature, or farther back than the present century, for a storehouse of great master-

pieces of the art. I have already spoken of
De Quincey and Carlyle. I know of no critic,
whether of literature or of painting, who, with
all his oddities, his waywardness, his egotism,
better repays an occasional visit than William
Hazlitt. What, for instance, can be better than
this sentence of his on Burke ?—" Johnson and
Junius shrink up into little antithetic points and
well-tuned sentences. But Burke's style was
forked and playful like the lightning, crested like
the serpent." Lamb and Coleridge, Bagehot,
Matthew Arnold, Stevenson, and that fine and
subtle writer whom we have lately lost and
cannot replace, Richard Holt Hutton, maintain a
succession which is carried on with undiminished
brilliancy by a band of living critics whom I need
not name. Familiarise yourselves with these
masters—with their temper, their method, their
style—and you will not lack the inspiration and
guidance which great models supply.

But it is, as the French say, by working at the
smithy that one becomes a blacksmith. One of
the acutest critics that I have known belongs to
the other sex, and if she did not acquire, she
certainly improved, her aptitude by the habit,
whenever she finished the reading of a book
which left its footprints behind it, of writing out
for herself a critical account of it. This is not
a bad practice, particularly if you find, as you
probably will, that the criticism of the first book

cannot be satisfactory to yourself until you have read round and about it, and your criticism insensibly widens into the study of a subject, a period, or an author. It is astonishing how continuously the resources are being increased upon which we can draw for the interpretation even of the most famous and most widely studied writers. We are met here on the anniversary of the birth of the greatest of them all. Shakespeare, both as writer and as man, has been the object of a more insatiable and a more microscopic criticism than any one in the generations of men. The most trivial episodes, real or imaginary, with which his name is connected, have been raked and sifted with Teutonic thoroughness. The " chatter about Harriet " is as nothing compared with the babel of tongues about " Mr. W. H." and Mary Fytton. And yet we have seen during the last twelve months three memorable contributions to our knowledge of Shakespeare and to our means of interpreting both his writings and his life—Mr. Sidney Lee's article in *The Dictionary of National Biography,* Mr. George Wyndham's Introduction to the *Poems,* and the monumental work of Dr. Brandes, which is now accessible to us all in an admirable English translation. The stream of criticism never runs dry, and there is no subject worthy of the serious study of men upon which the last word has yet been said.

I must now bring to a close these scattered hints on the study of the art of criticism. The criticism of literature and art is after all but a subordinate chapter in the criticism of life. In the ideal scheme of ancient philosophy, the life of action, immersed in matter, tinctured with passion, at its best but a halting compromise between the pure energies of reason and the more or less squalid exigencies of social co-operation, was always regarded as an indifferent second-best to the detached and isolated life of speculative thought. For us who pass our days *in Romuli faece*, the self-sufficing figure of the passionless and anaemic theorist, who seemed to Plato and Aristotle to be the fine flower of human development, has yielded the place of honour to that of the man who makes two blades of grass grow where only one grew before. It is a truism, but a truism which needs to be constantly repeated, that we are too apt in all departments to adjust our judgments to the vulgar modern rule of " payment by results." The disinterested pursuit of truth and beauty is always and everywhere the worthy goal of the best energies of the sons of men. In all ages and countries, under every condition of social and intellectual environment, those who have struggled, whether for the extension of the boundaries of knowledge or for the widening of the field of common refinement and general happiness, have always found

at the end of their journey that there still
lay before them and before those who were to
follow—

> that untravelled world, whose margin fades
> For ever and for ever when we move.

There is no intellectual formula that can express,
and no scientific crucible that can resolve, the
ultimate and irreducible secret either of our
individual or of our corporate life. But by close
and daily intimacy with the best that has been
thought and said we may nourish that temper
of " admiration, hope, and love," by which, as
Wordsworth tells us, we really " live."

II

BIOGRAPHY

II

BIOGRAPHY [1]

To the lover of books there are few more fascinating or more indispensable companions than the great *Dictionary of National Biography*, which, with the issue of its supplement, has just been brought (for the time being) to a close. The man who has on his shelves, and within easy reach, the sixty-six volumes of this monumental work need never be at a loss for intellectual nourishment and stimulus. Whatever may be his mood, grave or frivolous, strenuous or desultory, whether he wishes to graze, or, as one sometimes does, only to browse, he can hardly fail, as he turns over these infinitely varied pages, to find what fits his taste. Literature in our days tends to become more and more specialised; there are vast and ever-increasing tracts which are made inaccessible to the general reader by technicalities of dialect and of form; but in the written records of the lives of men and women we have all a common territory, inexhaustible

[1] Delivered at the Edinburgh Philosophical Institution, November 15, 1901.

in its range, perennial in its interest, from which pedantry itself cannot shut us out. It seemed to me, therefore, when the promise which, many months ago, I improvidently made to address the Edinburgh Philosophical Institution was at last coming home to roost, that I might do worse than speak to you this evening for a few moments on Biography as a form of literary art.

I do not propose to theorise at length upon the subject. It might, indeed, almost be said that the good biography, like the good biographer, is born, not made. There is no kind of composition for which it is more futile to attempt to lay down rules ; none in which it is more difficult *a priori* to say why one man should succeed, and another, with equal knowledge, better brains, and a readier pen, should ignominiously fail. We can easily enumerate a number of qualities, some of them commonplace enough, which the ideal biographer ought to possess—quick observation, a retentive memory, a love of detail, a dash of hero-worship. We can also say, negatively, that it is not the least necessary to the production of an immortal biography that the writer—or, for that matter, the subject either—should be a man of genius. But no theory, either of faculty, opportunity, or environment, will enable one to explain the supreme art, indefinable, incommunicable, which could create, say, such a masterpiece as Boswell's *Johnson*. Still, it may, I think, be worth while to endeavour, not as a mere speculation, but by the aid of concrete examples, to realise, if we can, some of the conditions which go to the making, and which account for the charm, of a good biography.

There is, I need hardly say, a wide difference, from the point of view both of the reader and the writer, between the summary and condensed record of a life in a dictionary, and a biography in the larger and fuller sense of the term. But, though the products of different literary methods, both depend for their interest upon their appeal to, and their satisfaction of, the same kind of intellectual curiosity. To the true lover of biography it matters comparatively little how much space the man of whom he is reading occupied in the eyes of contemporaries, or retains in the judgment of posterity. The interest of the life depends far more on the stature of the man than on the scale of his achievements. It must, nevertheless, be admitted that there is a peculiar fascination in trying to pierce through the gloom which veils the life-history of some of the most famous of our race.

To take an obvious, and at the same time an extreme, instance, few things are more interesting to watch than the attempts of scholars and critics, like Dowden and Brandes and Sidney Lee, to reconstruct the life of a man at once so illustrious and so obscure as the greatest of our poets.

The case of Shakespeare presents, perhaps, the strangest array of difficulties and paradoxes in the whole range of biography. The most splendid genius of his own or any other time has left behind him hardly a single undisputed trace of his own personality. There has not been preserved so much as a single line in his own handwriting of any of his poems or plays. Such of the plays as were published in his lifetime seem to have been printed from stage copies—to a large extent by literary pirates. The apparently unbroken indifference of the greatest of all artists not only to posthumous fame, but to the safeguarding against defacement or loss of his own handiwork, is without precedent or parallel. The date and order of his plays, the identity of the " only begetter " of the Sonnets, the manner in which his wealth was acquired, the unproductiveness of his last five years—he died at fifty-two, the same age as Napoleon—his easy acquiescence in the sleek humdrum and the homely dissipations of social and civic life in a small provincial town—that all these questions, and a hundred more, should still be matters of conjecture and controversy is a unique fact in literary history. What else but this tantalising twilight has made it possible for even the most distraught ingenuity to construct the great Baconian hypothesis ? The task which confronts the writer of a life like Shakespeare's is not to transcribe and vivify a record; it is rather to solve a problem by the methods of hypothesis and inference. His work is bound to be, not so much an essay in biography, as in the more or less scientific use of the biographic imagination. The difficulty is infinitely enhanced in this particular case by the impersonal quality of most of Shakespeare's writings—a quality which I myself am heretic enough to believe extends to by far the greater part of the Sonnets. We do not know that the greatest teacher of antiquity wrote a single line. Shakespeare, who died less than three hundred years ago, must have written well over a hundred thousand. And yet, thanks to Plato and Xenophon, we have a far more definite and vivid acquaintance with the man Socrates than we shall ever have with the man Shakespeare.

But dismissing problems of this kind, which have to be judged by a standard of their own, let me say a word first of that form of biography in which success is at once rarest and, when achieved, most complete — autobiography. It may, I think, be laid down, as a maxim of experience, without undue severity, that few autobiographies are really good literature. And the reason lies upon the surface. Self-consciousness is, as a rule, fatal to art, and yet self-consciousness is the essence of autobiography. No man ever sat down to write his own life, not even

D

John Stuart Mill, without becoming for the time an absorbed and concentrated egotist. It is because he is, for the moment at least, so profoundly interesting to and interested in himself, that he feels irresistibly impelled to take posterity into his confidence. The result too often is one of the most unappetising products of the literary kitchen—a nauseating compound of insincerity and unreserve. And yet in the hands of a true artist there is hardly any form of composition which has the same interest and charm. Even Dr. Johnson said that every man's life may best be written by himself. Take, for instance, that which is, I suppose, at once the most shameless and the most successful specimen of its class, the *Confessions* of Rousseau. His object, he tells us, was to show a man (meaning himself) in all the truth of nature, and his belief is (as he also avows) that no reader after going through the *Confessions* will be able to declare himself a better man than their author. It is amazing, at first sight, that he can imagine that such a belief will be able to survive the disclosure which he proceeds to make, of ungoverned impulse, of infirmity, and even of baseness. As Mr. Morley says : " Other people wrote polite histories of their outer lives, amply coloured with romantic recollection. Rousseau, with unquailing veracity, plunged into the inmost depths, hiding nothing that would be likely to make him either ridiculous or hateful in common opinion, and inventing nothing that could attract much sympathy or much admiration." Or again, in the words of Mr. Leslie Stephen, " he found realities so painful that he swore that they must be dreams, as dreams were so sweet that they must be true realities." And the same writer sums up his point of view in a sentence of singular felicity when he adds that " Rousseau represents the strange combination of a kind of sensual appetite for pure and simple pleasures." There are few more difficult questions than that which is constantly presenting itself to the reader of Rousseau, namely, what ought to be the limit of unreserve in autobiography, if indeed there ought to be any limit at all. You will remember how Boswell was rash enough on one occasion to say to Dr. Johnson, " Sir, I am sometimes troubled with a disposition to stinginess," and Johnson replied, " So am I, sir, but I do not tell it."

The great autobiographies of the world are to be found in many different shapes. Some of the best are spiritual and largely introspective, like Saint Augustine's *Confessions*, or Bunyan's *Grace Abounding*, or Newman's *Apologia*. Sometimes, again, they veil or colour under the form of fiction the personal experience of the writer, as in *Consuelo*, or *David Copperfield*, or *Villette*. Sometimes, without losing the note of egotism, they are frankly objective and mundane, as in the case of Benvenuto Cellini, and to a large extent of Gibbon. But all that are worthy of a place in this the highest class have one thing in common. They are authentic human documents—the very mirror of the writer's personality, and it is by that quality that they make an appeal to us, more vivid, because more direct, than any narrative by another hand.

I will not venture on any critical estimate of the famous works which I have just named. But let me take, by way of illustrating this branch of the subject, a less known, but, to my thinking, a hardly less remarkable book—the Autobiography of Benjamin Robert Haydon, the painter, one of the most tragic figures in the history of art. The gigantic canvases by which he confidently expected to achieve not only fame but immortality — his "Lazarus," which he sometimes thought his masterpiece, covers nearly 300 square feet—are perhaps as good an illustration as can be found of the difference between the grandiose and the great. He is probably best remembered in these days by Wordsworth's noble sonnet addressed to him as a fellow-worker in the school of "creative art "—

High is our calling, friend.

But Haydon, though cursed with a vain and violent temperament, a prey to ambitions always in excess of his powers of execution, perpetually hovering on the confines of the insanity to which he at last succumbed, was one of the acutest and most accomplished critics, and on the whole the most strenuous and indomitable controversialist of his time. In his journal and his unfinished autobiography he discloses to us his own personality with a freedom from reticence not unworthy of Rousseau, though you will look in vain in Rousseau or any of his imitators for Haydon's simplicity and sincerity. There is not a single phase of his experiences, from the day when he records how, at the age of eighteen, he left his home at Plymouth for London, full of buoyant self-confidence, down to the last pathetic entry, when, in front of his easel, and amid the wreckage of his ideals and his ambitions, he was about to take up the pistol with which he put an end to his life—in the whole of that long, strenuous, disheartening pilgrimage there is nothing that he thought, felt, did, or failed to do, that is not set down faithfully and without reserve. Haydon was an egotist, afflicted by an almost diseased vanity, but no reader can doubt the substantial truth of his picture of himself.[1]

---

[1] In 1846, two months before his tragic death, Haydon opened an exhibition of his pictures at the Egyptian Hall. But Tom Thumb, the American dwarf, proved a greater attraction. On April 21, Haydon notes in his diary: "Tom Thumb had 12,000 people last week. B. R. Haydon $133\frac{1}{2}$ (the $\frac{1}{2}$ a little girl)." Mr. Birrell recalls the lines:

> All London flocks to see a dwarf,
> And leaves a Haydon dying.

No picture of a man, however, whether by himself or by others, is either true or adequate which does not give us also his environment. It is here that so many autobiographies, being little more than the outpouring of self-consciousness, disappoint and baffle us. But here, again, Haydon appears to me to merit a high place. He is said to have been an indifferent painter of portraits with the brush. If he was, it was not, as these pages show, from a lack of power either to observe and remember superficial traits of appearance and manner, or—at least when his prejudices were asleep—to penetrate the depths of character. You will, I think, be grateful if I give you a few illustrations selected almost at random from a long and varied gallery. Here is a glimpse of two of his celebrated contemporaries — Hazlitt, the critic, and Jeremy Bentham, the philosopher. " What a singular compound," he says of Hazlitt, " this man was of malice, candour, cowardice, genius, purity, vice, democracy, and conceit. One day I called on him and found him arranging his hair before a glass, trying different effects, and asking my advice whether he should show his forehead more or less. Bentham lived next door. We used to see him bustling away in his sort of half-running walk in his garden. Both Hazlitt and I often looked with a longing eye from the windows at the white-haired philosopher in his

leafy shelter, his head the finest and most venerable ever placed on human shoulders. . . . Once
I remember," he goes on, " Bentham came to
see Leigh Hunt in Surrey Jail, and played battledore and shuttlecock with him. Hunt told me
after of the profound powers of Bentham's mind.
He proposed, said Hunt, a reform in the handle
of the battledore." No abuse was too vast, and
it would seem that no abuse was too small, to
escape the reforming passion of the great Utilitarian. Elsewhere he says of Hazlitt—and this,
I think, is a very remarkable picture : " As for
Hazlitt, it is not to be believed how the destruc-
tion of Napoleon affected him. He seemed pro-
strated in mind and body. He walked about
unwashed, unshaved, hardly sober by day, and
always intoxicated by night, until at length,
wakening as it were from his stupor, he at once
left off all stimulating liquors, and never touched
them after "—surely one of the quaintest occasions for taking the pledge in the whole history
of total abstinence.

Then, again, let me give you a portrait of
Wilkie, our great Fife painter, who was his fellow-
student, and his best friend through life. They
visited Paris together in 1814, after the first over-
throw of Napoleon. Haydon says that " not-
withstanding that Paris was filled with all the
nations of the earth, the greatest oddity in it
was unquestionably David Wilkie. His horrible

French, his strange, tottering, feeble look, his carrying about his prints to make bargains with printsellers, his resolute determination — here I seem to see something of the soil from which he sprang—never to leave the restaurants till he got his change right to a centime, his long disputes about sous and demi-sous with the *dame du comptoir*, while Madame tried to cheat him, and as she pressed her pretty ringed fingers on his arm without making the least impression, her ' Mais, monsieur,' and his Scottish ' Mais, madame,' were worthy of Molière." Or again, in a different vein, he tells us how he breakfasted with Wordsworth, and Wordsworth, speaking of three of the greatest men of his time, Burke, Fox, and Pitt, said : " You always went from Burke with your mind filled ; from Fox with your feelings excited ; and from Pitt with wonder at his having the power to make the worse appear the better reason." One is reminded of Porson's remark, that while Pitt carefully considered his sentences before he uttered them, Fox threw himself into the middle of his, and left it to God Almighty to get him out again.

Here is another of Haydon's sketches—the sketch of a money-lender—one of the fraternity to whom he paid in the course of his life a long series of unsatisfactory visits. This is his first experience. He says : " When you deal with a rascal, turn him to the light. I got him to the

light.   His eyes shrank, his face was the meanest
I ever saw ; the feeble mouth, little nose, brassy
eyes, blotched skin, low forehead, and fetid
smell all announced a reptile."   And afterwards,
when after a more extended experience of this
gentleman and his kind, he found himself at last
in the King's Bench prison, arrested for debt,
he writes—and this is characteristic of the man :
" King's Bench. Well ! I am in prison. So
were Bacon, Raleigh, and Cervantes."   He came
here to Edinburgh in 1821 to exhibit one of his
prodigious canvases, and it may be interesting
to you to know his first impressions of this great
city.   " The season in Edinburgh," he says,
" is the severest part of the winter.   Princes
Street in a clear sunset, with the Castle and the
Pentland Hills in radiant glory, and the crowd
illumined by the·setting sun, was a sight perfectly
original.   First you would see limping Sir Walter,
with Lord Meadowbank ;   then tripped Jeffrey,
keen, restless, and fidgety ;   you then met Wilson
or Lockhart, or Allan or Thompson, or Raeburn,
as if all had agreed to make their· appearance at
once."

Of Keats he writes : " The last time I ever
saw him was at Hampstead, lying on a white bed
with a book, hectic and on his back, irritable in
his weakness, and wounded at the way he had
been used.   He seemed to be going out of life
with a contempt of this world and no hope of

the other." Or, finally, to close my series of impressions from this storehouse of living portraits, take what he says of Scott and Wordsworth, who had spent the morning with him together : " It is singular how success and the want of it operate on two extraordinary men— Walter Scott and Wordsworth. Scott enters a room and sits at table with the coolness and self-possession of conscious fame ; Wordsworth with a mortified elevation of head, as if fearful he was not estimated as he desired. Scott is always cool and very amusing ; Wordsworth often egotistical and overwhelming. Scott seems to appear less than he really is, while Wordsworth struggles to be thought at the moment greater than he is suspected to be. I think that Scott's success would have made Wordsworth insufferable, while Wordsworth's failure would not have rendered Scott a whit less delightful. Scott is the companion of nature in all her feelings and freaks ; while Wordsworth follows her like an apostle sharing her solemn moods and impressions." I do not think it would be possible to present a more vivid contrast in fewer words between two great and distinguished men.

But I must leave autobiography and turn for a few moments to biography in the stricter sense —the writing of one man's life by another. In that form of literature no language is richer than ours ; it may be doubted whether any language is so rich. *Colonel Hutchinson's Life* by his wife, Roger North's *Lives of the Norths*, Boswell's *Johnson*, Lockhart's *Scott*, Carlyle's *Sterling*, Stanley's *Arnold*, Lewes' *Goethe*, Mrs. Gaskell's *Charlotte Brontë*, Trevelyan's *Macaulay*—these are only the titles which first suggest themselves in a brilliant and inexhaustible catalogue. Yet, with the single but large exception of fiction, there is no form of writing which lends itself so readily to the production of that which is trivial and ephemeral. It is hardly necessary to rule out, from the point of view of art, the monuments which filial piety or misdirected friendship is constantly raising to those who deserved and probably desired to be forgotten. Equally to be excluded, from the same point of view, is biography written with a purpose—a class of which those of us who were carefully brought up can recall not a few doleful specimens. Mr. Disraeli speaks somewhere, I think in *Coningsby*, of a voluminous history which once had a great vogue as " Mr. Wordy's History of the War, in twenty volumes, to prove that Providence was on the side of the Tories." The same taint of a perhaps laudable but certainly irrelevant purpose hangs about the didactic or edifying biography. It is not the function of a biography to. be a magnified epitaph or an expanded tract. Its business is the vivid delineation of a person, and for its success there are two obvious conditions—

first, that the person delineated should have the power of permanently interesting his fellow-men ; and, next, that the delineator should be able to recall him to life. The enormous increase, not only in the number but in the popularity of this class of books, is probably due more to the growth of the first class than the second. Man's interest in man is always growing, but from the nature of the case there is not and never can be an academy of biographers.

And here it may be worth noting that some of the most interesting personalities are the most elusive, and, therefore, the worst subjects for biography. There is about them a kind of bouquet which, after they are gone, can never be revived. For their friends, they may be brought back to life by the reminiscence of some slight, perhaps trivial, characteristic. It may be a trait or even a trick, a gesture, the inflexion of a voice, the turn of a phrase. But, for those who never knew them, not even the highest and subtlest art can reproduce them as they really were. We have all of us known such men. The late Master of Balliol, Mr. Jowett, was one. Lord Bowen, I think, was another. But let us suppose that the character and the life can be reproduced. What is the secret of the art which can make them live again ? Sometimes, of course, the biographer may be said not so much to recreate as to create his hero. One cannot help feeling a suspicion of the kind in reading a book like Carlyle's *Life of Sterling*. Sometimes, on the other hand, his function is exactly the opposite, and he is content to let his hero tell his own tale out of his own sayings or letters. An admirable example is Mr. Colvin's well-known edition of the *Letters of Stevenson*. The best selection of letters is, however, an inadequate substitute for a real biography. Indeed, one often feels that if we were given fewer of a man's letters to his friends, and more of his friends' letters to him, we should get to know him better because, among other reasons, we should be better able to realise how his personality affected and appealed to others.

Look for a moment to the list of famous Lives which I enumerated a little time ago, and you will find in them, at any rate, one common feature. With the single exception of Lewes' *Goethe*, there is not one of these great biographies which was not written either by a near relative or an intimate friend. The authors were, no doubt, all of them, in their degree literary artists ; but we can measure the enormous advantage to the biographer of personal intimacy when we compare the result of their own, or in some cases of still greater writers' attempts to bring back to life those whom they have never known in the flesh. " And did you once see Shelley plain ? " asks Robert Browning. To have " seen Shelley

plain " would have been, indeed, a godsend to
some of the accomplished gentlemen who have
contributed to " the chatter about Harriet."
The drawbacks of intimacy for this purpose are,
of course, sufficiently obvious. The bias of kinship, the blindness of discipleship, are undeni-
able hindrances to just and even-handed judgment. But the true biographer is not a judge.
He has no theory of his hero ; he presents him
to us as he appeared to those among whom he
acted and moved and suffered ; the living figure
of a man whom we feel we should recognise in
another world ; a figure, moreover, which is not
always the same, which grows and changes under
the stress of circumstance ; a figure which the
biographer, from his own store of direct knowledge, has, as it were, to be constantly recharging
with life. It is this quality which gives vividness,
charm, undying freshness to the pages of Boswell
and Lockhart. The biographer who has not this
advantage and has to seek for it elsewhere is
often in sore straits for the material which he
needs. Do you remember Dr. Johnson's account,
at Mr. Dilly's dinner, of his strenuous, but not
very successful, quest for authentic memories of
Dryden ? There were two people who had
known Dryden well still alive—M'Swinney and
Cibber. And what had they to tell ? M'Swinney's
only information was that " At Wills' coffee-
house Dryden had a particular chair set for him-

self by the fire in winter, and called his winter
chair, and it was carried out for him to the
balcony in summer, and then called his summer
chair." Cibber could only say : " He was a decent
old man, arbiter of critical disputes at Wills'."
There is no nutrition to be got out of chopped
straw like this. Boswell : " Yet Cibber was a
man of observation." Johnson : " I think not."

Let me again take by way of illustration not
a celebrated book, one which in these days has
probably few readers, a book in which a wife tells
the story of a man who was in his time a solid
and fruitful worker in business, in politics, and
in literature. I mean *The Personal Life of
George Grote*, by his widow, Harriet Grote,
published in 1873. Grote was not a genius, but
he was a man of many interests and activities—
a banker, for many years member for the City
of London, a politician who advocated with
serene and irrepressible courage unpopular
causes, and who at last, in despair at the inert-
ness of the public opinion of his time, abandoned
public life, devoted himself to research, and gave
up twelve years to writing *The History of Greece*.
Mrs. Grote, who was a woman of strong individuality, tells us in her preface how, late on
in his life, her husband one day came into her
room, and finding her poring over papers, asked,
" What are you so busy over, Harriet ? " " Well,
I am arranging some materials for a sketch of

your life." "My life!" exclaimed Grote, "there is absolutely nothing to tell." "Not in the way of adventure, I grant, but there is something nevertheless—your life is the history of a Mind." "That is it," he rejoined, with animation. "But can you tell it?" A conjugal query. But Mrs. Grote had no doubt about the answer, and proceeded with her task. Happily for its interest as a biography, the book is something very different from "the history of a mind." Even the great Goethe himself becomes barely endurable when he soliloquises over the stages of his own mental development.

Mrs. Grote had a keen eye, and the selective judgment which is peculiarly necessary when a wife undertakes to write the life of her husband. Grote fell early in life among the Utilitarians, and was brought in due course by James Mill to the feet of Jeremy Bentham. You have had one picture of the Patriarch already from the pen of Haydon. Here is a sidelight on the same subject from Mrs. Grote. "Mr. Bentham," she says, "being a man of easy fortune, kept a good table, and took pleasure in receiving guests at his board, though never more than one at a time. To his one guest he would talk fluently, yet without caring to listen in his turn." To this convivial monologue Mr. Grote seems now and again to have had the honour of being admitted. His engagement to Harriet Lewin, who became

his wife and biographer, was protracted by
business and other difficulties beyond the
ordinary span. He sought to appease his im-
patience by learning German, playing on the
'cello, and drenching himself with political
economy. I quote a typical entry, dated 1818,
from the diary which he kept for his lady :
" Dined alone. Read some scenes in Schiller's
' Don Carlos.' After reading these I practised
on the bass for about an hour. Then drank tea,
and read Adam Smith's incomparable chapter
on the Mercantile System until eleven, when I
went to bed." That is how the young Utilitarians whiled away their solitary evenings.
At last they married. Things were not at first
altogether easy. Mrs. George Grote, as she calls
herself, had, she tells us with delightful frankness,
" numerous friends and connections among the
aristocratic portion of society " ; but, as she says,
" the aversion at this early period of his life to
everything tinctured with aristocratic tastes and
forms of opinion which animated G. G.'s mind
obliged his wife to relinquish her intercourse
with almost all families of rank and position
rather than displease her (somewhat intolerant)
partner." Another drawback was—again to
quote her own words—that " the elder Mr. Grote
bore very little share in the labours of the banking
house during these ten years, but appropriated the
greater portion of the profits."

E

Mrs. Grote gives an animated narrative, which will not bear abridgement, of her husband's public life, with its strenuous labours and many disappointments, and of the tranquil and industrious later years, which were consecrated to scholarship and philosophy. It is full of vivid sketches of men and events, with not a few of those living touches which light up the past for us—as, for example, when she records that in 1837 Lord William Bentinck, the famous Governor-General of India, calling on her after a dinner-party, said : " I thought your American very pleasant company, and it was a surprise to me, for I never in my life before met an American in society." It would seem that the world gets rounder as the years roll on. In 1855 the twelfth and last volume of the great History was published, and Mrs. Grote determined to signalise the event. " I had," she says, " a bowl of punch brewed at Christmas for our little household at History Hut (Grote's workshop) in celebration of the completion of the *opus magnum*, Grote himself sipping the delicious mixture with great satisfaction, while manifesting little emotion outwardly."

This homely scene calls up, if only by way of contrast, the accounts which still greater writers than Grote have given of a like event in their lives. The passage in Gibbon's *Memoirs* is deservedly famous, but it will bear requoting : " It was

on the day, or rather night, of the 27th of June,
1787, between the hours of eleven and twelve,
that I wrote the last lines of the last page in a
summer-house in my garden. After laying down
my pen, I took several turns in a *berceau*, or
covered walk of acacias, which commands a
prospect of the country, the lake, and the
mountains. The air was temperate, the sky was
serene, the silver orb of the moon was reflected
from the waters, and all nature was silent. I
will not dissemble the first emotions of joy on
the recovery of my freedom, and perhaps the
establishment of my fame. But my pride was
soon humbled, and a sober melancholy was
spread over my mind, by the idea that I had
taken an everlasting leave of an old and agreeable
companion, and that whatsoever might be the
future fate of.my History, the life of the historian
must be short and precarious." Dr. Birkbeck
Hill, in his excellent edition of *Gibbon's Life*,
reminds us in this context of Carlyle's description,
in a letter to Emerson, of the completion of his
French Revolution : " You, I hope, can have
little conception of the feeling with which I
wrote the last word of it, one night in early
January, when the clock was striking ten, and
our frugal Scotch supper coming in. I did not
cry ; I did not pray ; but could have done both."
Grote sipping his punch, Carlyle sitting down
to his oatmeal, Gibbon pacing the acacia walk,

each having finished a task which had added a masterpiece to literature—these are figures which deserve to live in the memory.

In truth, the picture which we carry about with us of some of the most illustrious men is created, not so much by the rounded and measured story of their lives, as by a single act or incident or sentence which stands out from the pages, whether of the best or of the most inadequate biography. I think it is Boswell who quotes Plutarch to the effect that it is very often " an action of small note, a short saying, or a jest, shall distinguish a person's real character more than the greatest signs or the most important battles." It is so with Bentley, who lives by virtue of a single saying, to many who know little or nothing of the letters of Phalaris or the history of Trinity College. " It was said to old Bentley "—I am quoting from *The Tour to the Hebrides*—" upon the attacks against him— ' Why, they'll write you down.' ' No, sir,' he replied, ' depend upon it, no man was ever written down but by himself.' " Or take the notable answer of Bolingbroke, when it was suggested to him that he should make some rejoinder to the virulent assaults of Bishop Warburton : " I never wrestle with a chimney sweeper." Or, again (you will forgive for a moment, and not be unduly shocked by a bit of bad language), when on the field of Waterloo,

Lord Uxbridge, riding by the side of the Duke
of Wellington, lost his leg, the cannon shot which
struck him having passed first over the withers
of the Duke's charger, " Copenhagen " : " By
God, I've lost my leg," cried Uxbridge. " Have
you, by God ? " was all the Duke's reply. You
all remember the page in Lockhart which describes
how, on the occasion of George IV.'s visit to this
city, Sir Walter Scott, having claimed for his own
the glass in which the King had just drunk his
health, and reverently placed it in his pocket,
found on his return home that Crabbe had arrived
as his guest, and in his joy and excitement at
greeting the poet, sat down upon the royal
present, and crushed it into fragments. Could
anything be more characteristic of the man ?
Or—to take one other illustration from the
memories of this place—what can be at once more
illuminating and more pathetic than the last
words of Dr. Adam, the head of the High
School, who had numbered Scott himself, and
Brougham, and Jeffrey among his pupils :
" But it grows dark. Boys, you may go." It
is by seizing on incidents like these, small
in themselves, but revealing as with a sudden
flash the heights and depths of character, that
biography brings back to life the illustrious
dead.

Let me give you an Oriental apologue, which
is not beside the point. " I forbid you," said the

tyrannical Emperor to the Chief of the Tribunal of History, " to speak a word more of me." The Mandarin began to write. " What are you doing now ? " asked the Emperor. " I am writing down the order your Majesty has just given me." The Mandarin was a born biographer.

But I feel that I am becoming garrulous, and that it is time to bring to a close this desultory and far from philosophical discourse. Much has been left unsaid. Upon one vexed question in the ethics of biography, which was debated with much vehemence a few years ago, first over Mr. Froude's *Memoirs of Carlyle*, and then over Mr. Purcell's *Life of Cardinal Manning*, I will only remind you of Voltaire's saying : " We owe consideration to the living ; to the dead we owe truth only." The abiding interest of biography for each of us depends after all upon our estimate of the worth and reality of human life. Byron in one of his early letters—I quote from the new edition by which Mr. Prothero has laid all lovers of literature under a heavy debt—expresses in his characteristic way the cynical view : " When one subtracts from life infancy (which is vegetation), sleep, eating, and swilling, buttoning, and unbuttoning—how much remains of downright existence ? The summer of a dormouse." If so, the less said about it, the sooner it is forgotten, the better. But, in truth, it is because we all feel that life is to us the most serious of realities that we crave to know more of the lives of others. As Emerson says : " The essentials in it—youth and love, grief and action—we all share ; the difference of circumstance is only costume." And thus the reading of biography becomes something more than a form of literary recrea- tion. True, it furnishes the memory with a por- trait gallery of interesting faces. True, it makes history and philosophy and poetry vivid with the personalities of the men to whom we owe great causes, great systems, great thoughts. But it does more than this. It brings comfort, it enlarges sympathy, it expels selfishness, it quickens aspiration. " I console myself," says Emerson again, " in the poverty of my thoughts, in the paucity of great men, in the malignity and dulness of the nations, by falling back on these recollections, and seeing what the prolific soul could beget on actual nature. Then I dare ; I also will essay to be." And if at times we are tempted, as who is not ? to doubt the ultimate purpose and meaning of human existence, when we think of the millions of lives which deserve no record—lives " which came to nothing," lives full of " deeds as well undone "[1]—we must take refuge in the faith to which, in lines that ought not to die, Edward FitzGerald has given noble and moving expression :

---

[1] R. Browning, "A Toccata of Galuppi."

For like a child, sent with a fluttering light,
To feel his way along a gusty night,
Man walks the world : again, and yet again,
The lamp shall be by fits of passion slain ;
But shall not He who sent him from the door
Relight the lamp once more, and yet once more ? [1]

---

[1] Attar's "Bird Parliament."

III

ANCIENT UNIVERSITIES AND THE
MODERN WORLD

III

ANCIENT UNIVERSITIES AND THE
MODERN WORLD [1]

MY first duty to-day, and it is a most agreeable
one, is to express my heartfelt gratitude to the
students for the honour which they have done me
in choosing me as their Rector. I can conceive
of no man's ambition which ought not to be
more than satisfied with the affirmation, by such
a constituency, of his title to hold an office which
has been filled in the past (I omit the names of
those who are still alive) by such men as Burke
and Macaulay, Palmerston and Peel, Disraeli
and Gladstone. If I can make no claim—as I
certainly cannot and do not—to bend the bow
which has felt the touch of these giants of the
heroic age, I have special grounds for addressing
an appeal, which they did not need, to your kind
and indulgent consideration. Though an Englishman by birth and blood, I have now for more
than twenty years been a Scotsman by adoption.

[1] Rectorial Address delivered before the University of Glasgow, January 11, 1907.

Whatever opportunities I have had of serving the public, I owe first and foremost to the favour and confidence of the men of Fife ; and only in a less direct degree, to a great College at Oxford, which is a purely Scottish foundation, and which, as the illustrious names, among many others, of Adam Smith and William Hamilton attest, has for many generations been intimately allied with the University of Glasgow.

Oxford and Glasgow—there are hardly two cities in the world which in their history, their environment, all the conditions of their daily life, would appear to be more remote and less akin. The one still seems—as a gifted son of hers has said—to breathe from her towers and gardens the last enchantments of the middle ages ; the other, in her manifold municipal and industrial activities, is, perhaps, the most typical embodiment in the whole Empire of the spirit of modern progress. But in the things of which I propose to speak to you, there is between them, as I hope to show, by virtue of their Universities, a real intellectual and spiritual relationship.

My purpose is to consider what is the true service which in these days an ancient university can render to the modern world.

We start with the fact that our Universities, both English and Scottish, unlike most of our educational appliances, have not been brought into existence to supply modern needs, but are rooted in the past. There has been not a little controversy as to their historical origin. As I have had occasion to point out before, it is more than possible that the academic existence of Oxford and Cambridge was due in each case to a quarrel between Church and State. If it had not been for the controversy between Henry II. and Becket, and the consequent expulsion or recall of the large contingent of English students from Paris, Oxford might never have obtained the dignity of a *Studium Generale*. A little later, the strained relations between King John and the Pope seem to have been the cause which led a colony of fugitives from Oxford to find a new intellectual home in Cambridge. Here in Glasgow we date our beginnings from the famous Bull of the first of the ecclesiastical humanists, Pope Nicolas V., issued on the very eve of the fall of Constantinople, which may roughly be said to have ushered in what we call the Renaissance. But here, too, the real history of the University does not begin until Church and State fall out ; for it led a starved and struggling existence, until the suppression of the convents of the Mendicants in Reformation times provided it with the bare necessaries of life.

The mediaeval Universities had two charac-teristics which are to this day *articuli star':s aut cadentis Academiae*. In the first place, they were always in theory, and almost always in practice,

cosmopolitan. There were no barriers of birth
or class or fortune. The door was open to all.
Just as the Church was one and indivisible,
speaking one language, holding one creed, observ-
ing the same rites throughout Western Europe,
so, in the community of students and scholars,
there was a oneness of purpose and a comradeship
of speech and habit which transcended, though it
did not obliterate, racial and geographical distinc-
tions. The Scottish students, long before any
University had been planted in their own soil,
swarmed over Europe. They were to be found
in Paris, where they had a separate college ; in
Padua, where they had a Nation to themselves ;
and in almost all the academic towns of France,
Northern Germany, and of the Low Countries.
Scholars flocked to Oxford in the days of William
of Ockham and Roger Bacon from every part of
the Western World. The University of Bologna,
at the time when it held the first place among
the schools of Civil and Canon Law, is said to
have had no less than 20,000 students from
different countries. The Scottish Universities,
national as in a peculiar sense they have always
been, have in their turn exercised the same
hospitality, and have found room for outsiders
to whom Providence has denied the privilege of
being born on Scottish soil. When Adam Smith
lectured here in the middle of the eighteenth
century, quite a third of his class were Irish

dissenters, shut out by religious tests from their own Trinity College, and his fame attracted students not only from England, but from Geneva, and even from Russia. A less liberal policy prevailed in those days, not only in Dublin, but in Oxford and Cambridge, whose splendid endowments and great traditions were in danger of becoming—though they never in fact became —the exclusive property of a limited class. *Cuncti adsint* is the invitation addressed now, as always, to the world of students by every University that is worthy of the name.

But, further, the true University has always been not only cosmopolitan in its composition, but catholic in its range. A University such as yours never was, is not, and never ought to become, a technological institute for the creation and equipment of specialists. The modern student may smile at the scanty proportions of the mediaeval *trivium* and *quadrivium*. He may be tempted to scoff at the pettiness and futility of many of the problems upon which in those days Angelic and Invincible Doctors broke their teeth. The Latin of the Schoolmen is no doubt an uncouth jargon which smacks more of the Vulgate and the Corpus Juris than of Cicero or Livy. Their dialectics are monotonous and infertile, not because of any defect in their reasoning powers, or indeed in their logical apparatus, but because they were hedged in, both by authority and by ignorance, within the narrow boundaries of a single field. But whatever, within its confines, was knowable, they knew. It was said of Abelard, the forerunner of them all : *Illi patuit quicquid scibile erat.* The limits of the knowable —wherever they are to be placed—have in these days expanded so far that no ambition and no assiduity is equal to the task of taking all that lies within them for its province. Nothing can be more alien from the business of a University than to produce the shallow and fluent omni-science which has scratched the surface of many subjects, and got to the heart of none. But the fidelity of a University to the intellectual side of its mission must now, as always, be judged by the degree in which it has succeeded in enlarging and humanising the mental outlook of its students, and developing the love of knowledge for its own sake.

Such an ideal, I need hardly say, does not imply a divorce of knowledge from practice. Let me recall to your recollection a well-known and instructive incident in the history of this University. When James Watt in 1756 came back to Glasgow from London, the Corporation of Hammermen refused him permission to set up his business in the burgh, because he was neither son of a burgess nor an apprentice. The Faculty of Professors, of whom Adam Smith was one, at once appointed him mathematical instrument maker to the University, and gave him a room, as they had power to do, in the College buildings for his workshop. It was in this workshop—a favourite resort of Adam Smith — and while engaged on the repair of a model of a Newcomen engine belonging to the University, that Watt evolved the idea of the separate condenser. It is often out of the mouths of Professors, and at the hands of Universities, that the practical man learns for the first time the real meaning and the latent possibilities of his own business. States-men and financiers and industrialists have never received two more magnificent presents than the *Wealth of Nations* and the Steam Engine : and both came to them from within the walls of Glasgow College.

We may fairly remember such facts as these when the term " academic " is used, as it often is nowadays, as a label of reproach to designate a proposition or an argument which is otiose or fanciful—of which, at any rate, the practical man takes no account. I believe this to be an inde-fensible perversion of language. As Hazlitt says : " By an obvious transposition of ideas some persons have confounded a knowledge of useful things with useful knowledge." There is no fallacy which, in all its forms, a University is more bound by the very nature and object of its being to combat and expose.

I spoke a moment ago of the intellectual

F

stamp which a University ought to leave on those whom it teaches. But that after all is not the supreme or ultimate test of its work. In the long run, it will be judged not merely or mainly by its success in equipping its pupils to outstrip their competitors in the crafts and professions. It will not be fully judged even by the excellence of its mental gymnastic, or its contributions to scholarship and science. It will be judged also by the influence which it is exerting upon the imagination and the character; by the ideals which it has implanted and nourished; by the new resources of faith, tenacity, aspiration, with which it has recruited and reinforced the untrained and undeveloped nature; by the degree in which it has helped to raise, to enlarge, to enrich, to complete, the true life of the man, and by and through him, the corporate life of the community.

I shall not, therefore, be travelling beyond my province to-day, if I endeavour to illustrate by one or two examples the truth of a seeming paradox : the essential utility, nay, the indispensable necessity, from this wider point of view, of some of those forms of knowledge which the man of affairs is apt to discard as useless or superfluous, but which it is the prerogative duty of a University to keep alive.

Take, first of all, those literary studies to which a large part of the time and energy of this

and of other Universities continues to be given.
Nothing is easier than to belittle or disparage
their practical value. Nor will any one who is
acquainted, for instance, with the history of
scholarship deny that many of the hours and
days, and even years, which were devoted by
men of the type of Browning's Grammarian to
settling and unsettling and resettling the most
trivial minutiae, might have been almost as
profitably given to astrology or heraldry. " The
first distemper of learning," says Bacon in a
famous passage, " is when men study words and
not matter." He compares this " vanity " to
" Pygmalion's frenzy," and cites the leading case
of Erasmus. " Then did Erasmus take occasion
to make the scoffing echo : *Decem annos con-
sumpsi in legendo Cicerone*, and the echo answered
in Greek ὄνε, *asine*." [1]   The revival of learning in
Western Europe in the fifteenth century supplies
one of ·the best illustrations of this kind of
intellectual demoralisation. Neglect and contempt of literary form had reached their lowest
depth in the style of the later Schoolmen and
their pupils. It is humiliating to an Oxford man
to remember that, even in those bad days, the
Oxoniensis loquendi mos seems to have been a
byword for its slovenly incorrectness. Never
was transformation more rapid and complete.
Under the influence of the new passion for the

---

[1] *Advancement of Learning*, Book I.

ancient models, the study of words and style became for the time a religion. The Humanists were " intoxicated with the exuberance " of their new " verbosity." But it was a passing disease, and when it subsided the English of Cranmer, the German of Luther, the Italian of Dante and Petrarch and Boccaccio, had taken root, side by side with the classical languages, each to become the living source of a fresh and splendid progeny.

I will not enter upon the technical and singularly barren controversy as to whether literature or science affords the better training for the reasoning powers. There are some intelligences which no discipline can convert into accurately working instruments. And those which possess the capacity for being so developed vary as greatly in their structure and tendencies, and are therefore as little suited to a uniform regimen, as men's bodies and characters. No one will pretend that they ought all to be treated by the same method, unless he is either a quack, or possessed by that undiscriminating passion for symmetry, which used to make the Minister for Education in a neighbouring country reflect with complacency that, at a particular minute of a particular hour in the day, every schoolboy in every school in France was being confronted with the same fact in Roman History.

Nor shall I dwell, as an apologist for literary studies from the utilitarian point of view would

be well justified in dwelling, on the obvious
services which they render to the development
of the memory, the taste, and the faculty of
expression. The claim I make for them covers
much wider ground. The man who has studied
literature, and particularly the literature of the
Ancient world, as a student should, and as only
a student can—I am not speaking of those to
whom it has been merely a distraction or a
pastime—such a man possesses resources which,
if he is wise, he would not barter for a king's
ransom. He finds among men of like training
with himself a bond of fellowship, a freemasonry
of spirit and understanding, which softens the
asperities and survives the conflicts of professional or political rivalry. He need never be
alone, for he can, whenever he pleases, invoke
the companionship of the thinkers and the poets.
He is always annexing new intellectual and
spiritual territory, with an infinitude of fresh
possibilities, without slackening his hold upon
or losing his zest for the old. There is hardly a
sight or a sound in nature, a passion or emotion
or purpose in man, a phase of conduct, an achieve-
ment of thought, a situation in life—tragic or
comic, pathetic or ironical—which is not illumin-
ated for him by association with the imperishable
words of those who have interpreted, with the
vision and in the language of genius, the meaning
of the world.

Let me take another illustration from another branch of humane learning, which again, from the merely material point of view, may not seem to possess the quality of utility. I mean the study —the serious and scientific study—of History. Here, perhaps even more than elsewhere, both teacher and student are peculiarly exposed to the risks of specialism, and of the morbid excesses to which specialism leads—pedantry, want of perspective, over-emphasis of the unimportant, the passionate pursuit of small game which is not worth the efforts of the chase. There is, for instance, no better-attested fact in the history of the world—and few which are of less real moment—than that at some time, in or between the years 129 and 135 A.D., the Emperor Hadrian dedicated the Temple which, seven centuries after it was begun, he had brought to completion—the Olympieion at Athens. But a learned German writer has computed that there are no less than 130 different theories as to the precise date of the ceremony. The mind of the historical student is, indeed, in more danger than that of any other scholar of becoming a kind of Pantechnicon, in which every sort of furniture is heaped and packed together, instead of being a habitable home, where things useful and beautiful are arranged in their proper places, and in due relation to their special purposes.

But, if this peril is avoided, where can a man

find better nutriment, both for his intellectual and his moral judgment, than in watching the unfolding of the purposes of Providence in the long procession of men and events ? " Philosophy teaching by example," it has been called, and there is not an age nor a movement which has not a message of its own. Look for example at the reign of the Emperor Hadrian, of whom I spoke just now. In not a few of its aspects it has as good a title to be called the Golden Age as any era in history. It is certainly one of the times, if a man could select, say, half-a-dozen since the days of the Flood, in which he would be tempted to wish that he could have lived. It was an epoch of profound peace. Hadrian deliberately abandoned the uncertain conquests of his great predecessor Trajan, made no attempt to extend the boundaries of the Empire, and concentrated his whole efforts upon the task of bringing security, order, and the blessings of good administration, to the ninety millions of people over whom he reigned. In Pliny's fine phrase [1] the *immensa Romanae pacis majestas* covered the world, and gave it rest. Vast tracts of territory, Asia Minor, Syria, and a large part of North Africa, have never since enjoyed such happiness. Never at any time, before or since, has the area of civilisation been endowed with such a widely diffused wealth of works of art.

[1] Pliny, *Hist. Nat.* xxvii. 1.

Not to speak of Rome itself, Athens, Ephesus, Antioch, Smyrna, Carthage, Rhodes, Alexandria contained, each of them, treasures of architecture and statuary in a variety and abundance for which the whole world might now be ransacked in vain. The Museum of Alexandria—the earliest in date among Universities, and behind none of its successors in the magnificence of its endowments and the splendour of its traditions—was at the height of its activity and fame. Schools of learning were to be found in every part of the Empire. Hadrian himself—the most indefatigable of builders—established in the capital, which already contained more libraries and books than any other city, the Athenaeum which became the University of Rome.

The means of communication throughout practically the whole distance from the Solway to the Euphrates, were more perfect, and more freely and securely used, than at any subsequent time, until steam was applied to locomotion. No one put them more frequently or more severely to the test than Hadrian—a Reisekaiser, if ever there was one—the most restless, curious, and untiring of travellers. I have read somewhere that Sir Robert Peel, when, in the winter of 1834, he was summoned home from Italy by the King to form a Ministry, took exactly the same time in posting from Rome to London as the Emperor Hadrian had occupied in making the same journey seventeen hundred years before. "The acta diurna," says Professor Dill, "with official news and bits of scandal and gossip regularly arrived in distant provincial towns, and frontier camps. The last speech of Pliny, or the freshest epigram of Martial, were within a short time selling on the book-stalls of Lyons or Vienne." [1] The last of the considerable names in Latin literature belong to Hadrian's time : Juvenal, Suetonius, Martial, Statius, and (if he in fact survived Trajan) one greater than any of these—Tacitus.

And to turn from the world which he governed to the Emperor himself, we have in Hadrian, if one of the most inscrutable, certainly one of the most attractive and interesting figures in history. It may be doubted whether any ruler, possessing absolute and irresponsible power, ever devoted himself with more absorbing assiduity to the work of good government. To that work he brought great natural powers, a constructive and, at the same time, a rarely cultivated intelligence, an intense interest in literature and art, a genuine hatred of war and of all forms of cruelty and oppression, a singularly humane and tolerant temper, absolute freedom from

[1] *Roman Society from Nero to Marcus Aurelius*, by Samuel Dill, London, 1904, p. 205 : a masterpiece, if I may venture to say so, of scholarship, philosophic insight, and literary charm. Cf. *The Emperor Hadrian*, by F. Gregorovius, Eng. trans., London, 1898, and *The Silver Age of the Greek World*, by J. P. Mahaffy, Chicago and London, 1906.

ostentation or arrogance, an insatiable passion
for administrative reform. If there was, at the
same time, in his character a tincture of vanity
and of sensuality, a certain dilettantism in his
tastes, and, on the speculative side, an incon-
gruous and baffling blend of scepticism and
superstition, this is only to say that he did not,
and could not, transcend the conditions of his
age. Nothing can be more striking than the
contrast between his eager, full-blooded love of
the world and all its interests—his buoyant *joie
de vivre*—and the pessimism, the introspective
questionings, the unsatisfied yearnings, the unsleeping self-discipline, of the still greater man who
twenty years after his death succeeded to his office.
Hadrian is, in a sense, the Last of the Pagans.
Marcus Aurelius, among the occupants of thrones,
may fairly be called the First of the Saints.

And yet across this brilliant age were written,
as we now know, the letters of doom. " Death
is the lot of States just as it is of men," is a
saying of the great satirist of the next generation.[1]
Tacitus says of Nerva, that he was believed to
have reconciled two hitherto incompatible things
—despotism and liberty.[2] But that was a task
beyond the power even of a Hadrian. Of
political freedom not a vestige remained in Rome
itself, though the Emperor continued to show a

[1] Ἀποθνήσκουσι γὰρ καὶ πόλεις ὥσπερ ἄνθρωποι (Lucian, *Charon*, 23).

[2] . . . res olim dissociabiles miscuerit — principatum ac liber-
tatem (Tac. *Agricola*, c. 3).

conventional deference to the formal authority of the Senate. The free local life, which had lingered on in the provinces, was already on the wane, and its end was hastened by Hadrian's own organisation of a great Imperial service. And what of personal freedom ? Manumission had become a fashionable form of philanthropy ; the prolonged peace stopped the supply of captives who could be sold into servitude ; but it is computed by some authorities that still something like a third of the population of the Roman Empire were slaves. Society thus rested upon a foundation which was economically and ethically rotten.

What, again, can be more significant of the moral and religious atmosphere of the age than the almost universal acquiescence in the deification of Antinous, whose statues were to be found, and whose worship was practised, in all the chief cities of the Empire ? It was in vain that the great teachers, the stoic Epictetus, the eclectic Plutarch, preached, in terms which might often have been borrowed from the New Testament, of righteousness and self-suppression and even of judgment. They spoke to a generation which, in the midst of profound external order and tranquillity, of peace, of material comfort, of artistic refinement, was on the verge of spiritual bankruptcy. Over the whole scene, with all its brilliant superficial colouring, as Professor Dill says, there " broods a shadow . . . the swiftly stealing shadow of that mysterious eclipse, which was to rest on intellect and literature till the end of the Western Empire. It is the burden of all religious philosophy from Seneca to Epictetus, which was one long warning against the perils of a materialised civilisation." [1]

> The woods decay, the woods decay and fall. [2]

I have taken but one page out of a thousand in the book of history which might be cited to teach the same lesson. For the study of history brings us to the same conclusion as that of literature : that man does not, and cannot, live by bread alone.

Finally, I will ask you, in the few moments that remain, to take one further step with me. Literature, the expression of man's feelings and thoughts, his beliefs and hopes ; History, the record of his achievements and his failures ; Science, the ever-growing sum of his attempts to know, by hypothesis and experiment, the external conditions which determine his sensations and circumscribe his activity—each of these seemingly isolated efforts of the human intelligence proceeds upon presuppositions which are common to them all. But no student has got the full benefit of University teaching unless he has been led on to examine the presuppositions themselves. We say of propositions that one is

---

[1] Dill, *op. cit.* pp. 249-50.   [2] Tennyson, *Tithonus.*

true and another is false ; and the tests which
we are accustomed to employ as the criteria of
truth—conformity to some external standard,
self-consistency, adequacy as explanation, con-
gruity with the rest of our experience—vary
according to the subject matter with which the
proposition deals. But upon what does the
validity of *any* intellectual judgment finally
rest ? So, again, we say of an act that it is
right or wrong, and there is general consensus
as to the practical application of the terms. But
whence is the authority of the moral imperative
derived ? And then there emerges, equally insist-
ent, the larger and deeper question still : whether,
in the flux of phenomena, there is discoverable by,
or revealed to, man any ultimate basis of Reality ?

These things may not, and do not, trouble the
man in the street, but they have supreme interest
and urgency for those who take thought seriously.
Nowhere do we stand in greater need of courage
and honesty : courage, not to shirk problems, by
trying to believe that they do not exist ; honesty,
in facing solutions, whatever may be their consequences. You cannot get rid of the debt which
you owe to yourself and the world as a sentient
and self-conscious personality—a " being of large
discourse, looking before and after "—by a simple
declaration of insolvency.

We have all known men of lofty courage and
inflexible honesty who, in the pursuit of these

inquiries, have been driven to the conclusion that the highest categories of experience are illusions ; that the boundaries of the knowable are drawn just where the human spirit craves for more and fuller light ; that beliefs which cannot be measured by some material calculus must be dismissed as superstitions ; except, perhaps, the sunless creed which

> . . . thanks with brief thanksgiving
>   Whatever gods may be
> That no life lives for ever,
> That dead men rise up never ;
> That even the weariest river
>   Winds somewhere safe to sea.[1]

But it is not in that direction that the best philosophic teaching of our age is tending. The enormous material development of the last thirty years has been accompanied, in the sphere of thought, especially among the English-speaking peoples, by a growing revolt against the ascendency of intellectual and spiritual Nihilism. Thirty years and more ago, when I was at Balliol, my own great teacher, Thomas Hill Green—*clarum et venerabile nomen*—and his friend and fellow-worker, Edward Caird, whom Glasgow has since sent to the Mastership of my old College, were almost solitary voices in the opposite sense. But the Time Spirit was working with them, and the living thought of to-day declares, with an ever-

[1] Swinburne, *The Garden of Proserpine*.

swelling emphasis, that there is a solid and
unshakable basis, in the very nature and conditions of our experience, alike for knowledge, for
conduct, and for worship.

What then is the sum of the whole matter ?
For the moment you here can concentrate yourselves on the things of the mind, installed as you
are in the citadel of knowledge.

> νέον νέοι κρατεῖτε, καὶ δοκεῖτε δὴ
> ναίειν ἀπενθῆ πέργαμ'.[1]

But after these student years are over, the
lives of most of us are doomed to be immersed
in matter. If the best gift which our University
can give us is not to be slowly stifled, we must
see to it that we keep the windows of the mind,
and of the soul also, open to the light and the
air. We must take with us into the dust and
tumult, the ambitions and cares, the homely joys
and sorrows, which will make up the texture of
our days and years, an inextinguishable sense of
the things which are unseen, the things which
give dignity to service, inspiration to work,
purpose to suffering, a value, immeasurable and
eternal, to the humblest of human lives.

Provided we live in this temper and spirit, it
matters comparatively little whether we take a
high or low view of what men's efforts can
actually achieve. There is a noble optimism
which, in spite of all disappointments and mis-

[1] Aeschylus, *Prom.* 954-55.

givings, holds fast to the faith in what man can do for man. There is also a noble pessimism, which turns in relief from the apparent futility of all such labour to a keener study and a fuller understanding of the works of God. I cannot better illustrate the difference, or more fitly finish what I have to say to you to-day, than by setting side by side two of the greatest utterances of two of our greatest writers—the prayer of a soiled and worldly statesman, who was yet a monarch of thought, and the aspiration of an unsoiled and unworldly dweller in untrodden ways, who was yet supreme in spiritual insight among poets. The prayer is that of Bacon, on the threshold of his *Instauratio Magna* : " Tu postquam conversus es ad spectandum opera quae fecerunt manus tuae, vidisti quod omnia essent bona valde ; et requievisti. At homo, conversus ad opera quae fecerunt manus suae, vidit quod omnia essent vanitas et vexatio spiritus ; nec ullo modo requievit. Quare si in operibus tuis sudabimus, facies nos visionis tuae et sabbati tui participes." [1] The aspiration is that of Wordsworth, in the last of his Sonnets on the River Duddon :

> Still glides the Stream, and shall for ever glide;
> The Form remains, the Function never dies;
> While we, the brave, the mighty, and the wise,
> We, Men, who in our morn of youth defied

---

[1] *Instauratio Magna : Distributio Operis, ad fin.*

The elements, must vanish;—be it so!
Enough, if something from our hands have power
To live, and act, and serve the future hour;
And if, as toward the silent tomb we go,
Through love, through hope, and faith's transcendent
    dower,
We feel that we are greater than we know.[1]

---

[1] *The River Duddon*, Sonnet XXXIV. "After-Thought."

IV

CULTURE AND CHARACTER

IV

CULTURE AND CHARACTER[1]

MY first duty is to thank you most gratefully for
the honour which the students of this University
have done me in electing me to be their Rector,
and to express my sincere regret that the pressure
of other duties has delayed so long my visit to
Aberdeen. The office to which you have elected
me is associated with some of the most splendid
traditions in the history of learning. It goes
back to the time when the Church and the
Empire, in theory at any rate, exercised an
unchallenged supremacy over the spiritual and
temporal concerns of the Western World. Three
out of our four Scottish Universities are of Papal
foundation. Aberdeen, the youngest of the three,
owes its origin in 1494, as you all know, to a
Bull of Alexander VI., which may, I suppose,
be regarded as a redeeming act in the career of
one of the most infamous of the Popes. It was,
at any rate, the final gift of the Papacy to learning
and the humanities in this island. For of the

[1] Rectorial Address delivered before the University of Aberdeen, October 25, 1910.

two great disruptive forces—the Renaissance and
the Reformation—which within the next half-
century undermined and overthrew the spiritual
and ecclesiastical unity of Europe, the one had
already begun its invasion of Great Britain, and
both in England and Scotland, by diverse routes,
the way was being prepared for the triumph
of the other. But in neither country ought we
to erase from the national memory the debt of
obligation which British learning owes to the
great Churchmen of the Middle Ages—a debt
which, I am glad to know, we here in Aberdeen
are about to recognise by a fitting commemora-
tion of our real founder, Bishop Elphinstone.

When we look back to the way in which organ-
ised education has been developed in Western
Europe, and particularly in Great Britain, we
are struck by the fact that it apparently began
at the top of the scale with the more advanced
forms of teaching. In point of time, you have
first the Universities, then what we call in England the public schools and the grammar schools,
and, finally, the parish school, which the whole
English-speaking world owes, in so large a degree,
to the insight and foresight of John Knox. We
must, however, not be misled into wrong infer-
ences, which may easily be drawn from a superficial survey of the facts. The mediaeval University was never intended to be, and was not
in fact, an aristocratic or exclusive institution,

which opened its doors and offered its teaching
only to the children of the well-to-do.   As I
tried to show some years ago, when on a similar
occasion to this I was addressing your fellow-
students at Glasgow, the typical University of
the Middle Ages, whether at Paris, or Bologna,
or Oxford, was cosmopolitan in composition ;
to some extent at any rate—as this institution
of the Rectorship proves—democratic in government, and recruited by students drawn from
all ranks and classes, but for the most part the
sons of low-born or needy parents.   University
education was then—except, of course, for the
few who pursue learning for learning's sake, and
who are, at all times, in every home of learning,
a minority of a minority—the most accredited
qualification for admission to, and for the practice
of, certain indispensable and much-frequented
professions—in particular, the Law, and the
higher branches of Medicine, and the Church.

As time went on, and the so-called ages of
Chivalry were submerged by the Renaissance,
what we now describe as culture, in the academic
sense, came to be looked on as the proper and
necessary accomplishment of a gentleman.   It
is true (as Mr. Sidney Lee has pointed out in the
learned and interesting book, which he has just
published, on *The French Renaissance in England*)
that the process was slower in this island than
elsewhere.   More, Colet, Linacre, and their

teacher and friend Erasmus, sowed the seed which did not ripen for harvest until Elizabeth had been more than twenty years on the throne. But the illustrious Queen herself, according to the unimpeachable testimony of the younger Scaliger, was better educated than all her contemporaries among the great of the earth, being familiar with no less than five languages in addition to her native tongue—Latin and Greek, French, German, and Italian. I hesitate to trespass, even for a moment, upon thorny ground, but with all the progress that female education has made in the last three centuries, can it produce a more conspicuous example of the combination of culture and capacity ?

Culture, as I have said, came to be looked upon, like good manners and good clothes, as part of the social and personal equipment of the well-born and well-to-do. It continued also, in its more specialised forms, to be the recognised avenue to eminence in the learned professions and the Church. But the notion that education was for the common man a part of his natural heritage, a necessary condition of his civic usefulness, an ingredient that could be safely mixed with the drudgery of manual toil and the simple round of homely pleasure—except, indeed, to some extent in Scotland—such a notion would have been everywhere dismissed as a dangerous paradox.

It is a little more than a hundred years since

an eminent prelate of the Church of England
declared that all that the people of a country had
to do with its laws was to obey them.   It was in
the same spirit, and from the same point of view,
that the mass of the population was expected
to leave letters to their betters.   The growth
of enlightenment, a stimulated sense of social
community and corporate duty, and, it must be
added, the advent of democracy, have brought
about, without violence, and by general consent,
the most revolutionary of all the changes of our
time—a national system of free and compulsory
teaching.   The celebrated sarcasm of Mr. Lowe,
that we must begin to " educate our masters,"
has been translated into practice ; and though
there are still plenty of ragged edges and ugly
gaps in the actual working of the machinery,
the ideal, at any rate, is universally accepted,
that no child shall start upon the work of life
unfurnished with the keys of learning, and that,
in the case of every child whom nature has gifted
with brains and ambition, the barriers of fortune
and circumstance shall no longer block its progress, at any stage of the way which leads to the
innermost courts of the palace of knowledge.
This is not an appropriate time or place to discourse, as I might otherwise be tempted to do,
on the lights—and shadows—of popular education.   It will be more to the purpose if I ask
your patience for a few desultory and discursive

thoughts on some of the shortcomings and drawbacks which seem in these days to threaten the academic pursuit of the higher forms of knowledge.

I would instance, first, the growing tendency
to Specialism, which has become a marked
feature of University work, both here and in
England, during the past fifty or sixty years.
It is much more common than it used to be for
a student to give exclusive, or almost exclusive,
devotion to one subject or group of subjects,
and to be content as regards the rest with the
bare minimum of academic requirement. The
change is, of course, largely due to the greater
thoroughness with which each subject is taught
and learnt ; to the enormous extension in the
area of the fields of research, which are still
called by the old names—classics, mathematics,
science, philosophy ; to the higher standard,
both of information and of exactness, which has
naturally and legitimately been set up. All this
is to the good, in so far as it tends to promote
erudition and accuracy at the expense of that
which is merely superficial and smart. But the
advantage is purchased at an excessive price if
it is gained by the sacrifice of width of range
and catholicity of interest. Pedantry is, on
the whole, more useful and less offensive than
Sciolism, but a University which is content to
perform the office of. a factory of specialists is
losing sight of some of its highest functions.

Nobody but an impostor can in these days assume to take all knowledge for his province. Such an encyclopaedic purpose as inspired Francis Bacon, even he, perhaps the most gifted of our race, if he could be reincarnated under modern conditions, would recognise to be now beyond the dreams of intellectual ambition. But the man whom you turn out here as your finished product at the end of his University course ought to be, in Bacon's own phrase, a " full man." Victor Hugo says somewhere, in his grandiose and impressive way, that genius is a promontory which stretches out into the Infinite. We cannot lay down laws for genius ; that incommunicable gift sets at nought both heredity and environment. But, genius apart, there is much to be said for the old University ideal of the " all-round " man—not the superficial smatterer, who knows something about everything and much about nothing—but one who has not sacrificed to the pursuit of a single dominating interest his breadth of outlook, the zest and range of his intellectual curiosity, his eagerness to know and to assimilate the best that has been and is being thought and written and said about all the things that either contribute to the knowledge or enrich the life of man.

But, next, if a certain width of range is essential to the reality of academic culture, it is equally true that, in external form and expression, it is, or ought to be, marked by precision, aptitude, harmony—by the qualities, in a word, which combine to make up what we call Style. In all artistic production there are three factors—the subject, the form in which it is presented, and the vehicle by which the presentation is effected. In each of the separate arts—painting, sculpture, architecture, music—the particular vehicle controls and limits the choice of subject. But given appropriate subject and apt vehicle—and there is nothing in which the insight of genius is better tested than in the mating of the two—it is the formative capacity of the artist which determines the value of the product. That sounds like a platitude when we are talking of the fine arts ; but it is strange how careless of form even highly educated people show themselves in the commonplace everyday acts of speaking and writing. A vast deal of the slipshod and prolix stuff which we are compelled to read or to listen to is, of course, born of sheer idleness. When, as so often happens, a man takes an hour to say what might have been as well or better said in twenty minutes, or spreads over twenty pages what could easily have been exhausted in ten, the offence in a large majority of cases is due, not so much to vanity, or to indifference to the feelings of others, as to inability or unwillingness to take pains.

And the uncritical world, just as it is apt to

mistake noise of utterance for firmness of character, has an almost invincible tendency to think
that a writer or orator cannot be eloquent unless
he is also diffuse. In my opinion, it ought to
be regarded as one of the serious functions of
a University to inculcate the importance and to
cultivate the practice of Style. Remember that
in the English language we have received, as
part of our common inheritance, the richest and
most flexible organ of expression among living
tongues. I say nothing for the moment of
Poetry, which may be classed among the arts ;
but there is no department of the Prose, which
we all have to speak and write every day of our
lives, for which our literature does not provide
us with a wealth of models and examples. There
are fashions in style, as in other things, which
have their day, exhaust themselves, and cannot
be revived. No one, for instance, would nowadays set himself deliberately to copy the manner
of Archbishop Cranmer, the first great writer of
English prose ; or of Sir Thomas Browne, with
his magnificent organ of many notes ; or of
Gibbon, who stands in solitary splendour at the
head of our writers of history ; or of De Quincey,
with his curious and sometimes irritating medley,
imaginative, critical, discursive, but a master
who has rarely been surpassed in the manipulation
of the English sentence. Mechanical reproduc-
tion may be useful as an exercise ; it was resorted

to, if I remember right, in his youth by the most
accomplished practitioner in the art of style that
Scotland has produced in our time — Robert
Louis Stevenson. But the man who wants to
write or speak English will go to the great
authors, whom I have just named, again and
again; not to echo their cadences or to mimic
their mannerisms; not merely even to enrich
his own vocabulary; but to study the secret of
their music; to learn how it is that, with
them, language becomes the mirror of thought;
to master, step by step, the processes by which
these cunning artificers in words forge out of
them phrases, sentences, paragraphs, and give
to each its proper place and function in the
structure of an immortal work.

But, further, it is not enough that a University
should teach its students to eschew narrowness
in the range of their intellectual interests and
slatternliness in speech and writing. It should
put them permanently on guard against the
Dogmatic temper. We cannot get on without
dogma, which is nothing more than the precisely
formulated expression of what we believe to be
true. The term is sometimes used as though it
were restricted to the domain of theology, and
were specially appropriate to the accretions—
called by some excrescences, by others developments—which councils and schoolmen and
doctors have embroidered upon the simplicity

of the Gospel. But science and philosophy have
their dogmas also ; and if it be suggested that
that which differentiates a dogma is that it is
accepted in deference, not to reason, but to
authority, the same may be said of not a few of
the propositions which in every department both
of speculation and of practical life form the basis
of belief or conduct. But to give intellectual
acceptance to a dogma, or a series of dogmas,
is one thing; to carry on the operations of the
intellect in a dogmatic spirit is quite another.
There is a famous and familiar saying of Lessing,
that if the Almighty offered him the choice
between the knowledge of all truth and the
impulse to seek the truth, he would reverently
select the second as a greater boon than the first.
And this surely is the attitude which it should be
the aim and end of education to make easy and
natural.   To be open-minded ; to struggle against
preconceptions, and hold them in due subjection;
to keep the avenues of the intelligence free and
unblocked ; to take pains that the scales of the
judgment shall be always even and fair ; to
welcome new truths when they have proved their
title, despite the havoc they may make of old
and cherished beliefs—these may sound like
commonplace qualities, well within every man's
reach, but experience shows that in practice
they are the rarest of all.

The temper which I am endeavouring to

describe is not in any sense one of intellectual detachment or indifference ; nor has it anything in common with that chronic paralysis of the judgment, which makes some men incapable of choosing between the right and wrong reason, or the better and the worse cause. It implies, on the contrary, an active and virile mental life, equipped against the fallacies of the market-place and the cave, animated by the will to believe and to act, but open always to the air of reason and the light of truth.

One final counsel I will venture to offer to you. I speak as an old University man who, in a crowded and somewhat contentious life, has never wholly lost touch with the interests and the ideals of Oxford days. If the short span which, in fuller or lesser measure, is allotted to us all is to be wisely spent, one must not squander, but one should husband and invest, what never comes again, and what here and now is offered to every one of you. The more strenuous your career, the more you will need to draw upon that unfailing reservoir. Sometimes, amid the clash of public strife, there may steal back into the memory of some of us the sombre lines of the greatest of Roman poets :

Di Jovis in tectis iram miserantur inanem
Amborum, et tantos mortalibus esse labores.

That is but a passing mood, except in an ill-furnished mind. Keep always with you, wher-

ever your course may lie, the best and most
enduring gift that a University can bestow—
the company of great thoughts, the inspiration
of great ideals, the example of great achievements,
the consolation of great failures. So equipped,
you can face, without perturbation, the buffets
of circumstance, the caprice of fortune, all the
inscrutable vicissitudes of life. Nor can you do
better than take as your motto the famous words
which I read over the portals of this College
when I came here to-day : " They have said.
What say they ? Let them say."

V

THE SPADE AND THE PEN

V

THE SPADE AND THE PEN [1]

THAT it is my privilege as President for the
year of the Classical Association to deliver my
address to its members assembled in the Town
Hall of Birmingham may be regarded, I think,
as a striking illustration of the interdependence
in this country of culture and practice.

Birmingham, among all English towns, is
perhaps the one most associated in popular
thought and speech with the strenuous interests
of business and politics. I myself, for a long time
past, have been compelled to spend my waking
hours—if I may use an ancient phrase without
offence—*non in Platonis republica sed in Romuli
faece*. But Birmingham has set up a University
—which of us does not feel to-night the gap on
our platform due to the much-regretted absence
of its illustrious Chancellor, Mr. Chamberlain ?
—a University with a Faculty of Arts, and a
Professor of Greek and Latin in the person of

[1] Presidential Address delivered before the Classical Association, Town Hall, Birmingham, October 9, 1908.

Dr. Sonnenschein, who has been a pioneer of useful experiments in the art of teaching the ancient languages, and has done as much as any one to organise and develop the work of the Classical Association. And although, when I remember that I am in the chair which was occupied by Dr. Butcher, I am painfully sensible that one who is not even worthy to be called a scribe has stolen into Moses' seat, yet I can honestly say that I have never wavered in my allegiance to the great writers of antiquity, or ceased to take a lively interest in the progress of criticism and discovery which is every year throwing new light on their meaning, and laying deeper and broader the foundations of their imperishable fame.

The Classical Association has a double side to its activities. It seeks to examine and improve our English methods of studying and teaching the Classics. It seeks also to co-ordinate and bring together the ever-accumulating results of the labours of British and foreign scholars. Under the first head it has already, in the course of two years, brought about a radical change, which, both in the magnitude of its scale and the rapidity of its execution, may well excite the envious admiration of iconoclasts and revolutionaries in other walks of life. The reformed scheme of Latin pronunciation has been adopted, and is in practical use in our Universities and in most, if not in all, of our public schools. It was recommended for use in secondary schools by the Board of Education in a circular issued in February 1907, which, however, left it open to the schools to retain if they pleased the traditional English pronunciation. It will be interesting to you to know the results, the details of which will be set out in the forthcoming Report of the Board. Broadly speaking, it may be said that the use of the reformed pronunciation has become normal in grant-earning schools. Returns have been received from 577 schools in which Latin is taught. Of these, no less than 550 use the reformed pronunciation. In 24 out of the 550 the scheme of the Association has been adopted with modifications of one kind or another, those most commonly made being (1) the distinction between u the vowel and v the consonant, and (2) the retention of the traditional English consonantal sounds—as, for instance, the soft c and g before the vowels e and i. You have thus, in effect, in the course of two years made a clean sweep of a system of mispronunciation which has prevailed in this country for more than three centuries, and which has done not a little to isolate English scholarship. Encouraged by this success, the Association is now attacking the problem of the pronunciation of Greek. It will be interesting to see whether, in this more broken and difficult ground, it will be found equally easy to rout the forces of conservatism.

Side by side with these large reforms, the Association is prosecuting a less ambitious but equally useful task in seeking to secure that the highest educational value shall be got out of the time which is given in most English schools to the teaching of Latin. It is satisfactory to observe that the best authorities, even those who speak in the name of natural science, are practically unanimous as to the necessity of retaining the study of Latin. When one remembers how few of those who at present are learning Latin in school can by any possibility develop into scholars in any real sense of the term, it is obviously of the first importance that Latin should be taught in such a way as to be a propaedeutic, and a real intellectual discipline. Too often in the past the only permanent mental gain from the hours devoted during many years to the learning of Latin has been one of at least dubious value—a good memory for what is trivial and just as well forgotten.

But, as I said just now, the Association has charged itself with another function—that of bringing together in a coherent and connected form, from time to time, the results of the researches and discoveries of those who are engaged in the different fields of scholarship. How many those fields are, how indefinitely varied is their yield, and yet how important it is that the work done in each should be brought

into reciprocal relation with the work done in all
the rest, will become at once apparent to any one
who looks at the admirable annual compendium
which is edited for the Council by Dr. Rouse.
The subjects treated are indeed almost bewilder-
ing in their number and diversity. Archaeology
in all its ramifications, Sculpture, Numismatics,
Mythology, Epigraphy, History, Grammar,
Textual Criticism — even this comprehensive
catalogue by no means exhausts the various
forms of activity which the learned of all countries
are devoting every year to a better and closer
knowledge of the ancient world. It is a perusal
of this volume which has suggested to me one or
two reflections on the changes which within my
own memory, and that of many here present, have
been brought about in this country both in the
conception and the practice of classical study.

Let me make my meaning clear by an illustration. I was reading the other day a discourse
delivered to the Classical Association of Scotland
by Professor Ridgeway, whose *Early Age of
Greece* has laid me, among many others, under
a deep debt of obligation. Its subject is the
relation of archaeology to classical studies. His
main thesis appears to be that, after the death
of Porson, English scholarship rapidly degener-
ated into pedantry and verbalism, of which the
highest achievements were a happy guess at a
new reading in a corrupt passage, or some *tour*

de force in the elegant and futile trivialities of Greek and Latin versification.

If, as he appears to hold, the field has now been broadened, and English scholarship has recovered, or is recovering, its sense of proportion, the result is in his opinion largely to be attributed to the introduction and acknowledgment of archaeology as a necessary part of the scholar's equipment. I think that Professor Ridgeway is a little disposed to underestimate both the range and the productiveness of classical scholarship in this country, in what I may call the pre-Schliemann era, when practically all that we knew of the early history of Mycenae and Crete was to be found in the *Iliad* and the *Odyssey*. Yet these were the days in which, to mention only a few out of many possible examples, such books as Munro's *Lucretius*, Conington's *Virgil*, Jowett and Thompson's editions and translations of Plato, and the earlier part, at any rate, of Jebb's *Sophocles*, saw the light. But there can be no doubt that Schliemann and his successors have had what can only be described as a revolutionary influence, and have to some extent altered the bearings of English and indeed of universal scholarship. During the last twenty years it is hardly an exaggeration to say that in this domain the pen has become the servant of the spade. We now know that the pre-Homeric civilisation, of which nearly the first traces were unearthed

at Mycenae and Tiryns and Hissarlik, stretches
back into an almost immeasurable past. It may
be, and probably is, the case that it went through
stages of development and decadence in the
Cyclades and Crete before it crossed to the
Argolid. Mr. Evans and his school believe that
they can trace no less than eight so-called
Minoan epochs, each with a characteristic art of
its own, before they reach the era called Late
Minoan III., which begins with the sack of the
later Palace at Knossos about 1400 B.C., and
which, corresponding roughly with the so-called
Mycenaean of the mainland, perhaps lasts to
1000 B.C. The revelation of the existence during
centuries, possibly during thousands of years,
of this almost unsuspected Aegean world, has,
of course, compelled a revision of the traditional
notion, in which most of us were brought up, that
we have in the Homeric poems the first records
of historic Greece. There is, no doubt, much
that is still obscure, and, if I may venture to say
so, still more that is highly conjectural, in the
picture which Archaeology has constructed of
what may be called, without prejudice, the pre-
Achaean ages. The great Palace at Knossos, in
its wall decorations and in its sanitary and
hydraulic arrangements, was rarely, if ever,
surpassed in the later days of Greek art. We
gather from that which remains of their art that
the men who erected and lived in and about

this wonderful building were a dark-skinned and long-headed race, with shaven faces, short in stature and narrow in waist, who were still in the bronze age, and who buried and did not burn their dead. Their language does not help us, for, as I understand, none of the Cretan scripts, whether pictographic or linear, have as yet been satisfactorily deciphered. Can they be properly described as a Greek race? Is their art to be called Greek Art? In the successive waves of migration, of which the origin, the succession, and the effect seem to become more rather than less disputable with the progress of research, were they swept out of existence or absorbed either as a dominant or a contributory factor in the historic Hellenic race? To these questions Professor Burrows, who has collected in his excellent book [1] everything that is relevant to the subject, admits that at present no definite answer can be given.

Prehistoric archaeology in the region of the Aegean has indeed raised more questions than it has solved. To say this is not to disparage or undervalue the service which it has rendered, particularly to Homeric scholarship—in correcting crude theories, in setting aside false interpretations, in giving historic actuality to what used to be regarded as manifestly legendary or fictitious, and generally in recasting the perspective of the

[1] *The Discoveries in Crete*, by R. M. Burrows. London: John Murray, 1908.

Poems. But to the student of ancient literature, archaeology (as Professor Ridgeway rightly says) must be kept in an ancillary position. It must not occupy the foreground and dominate the scene. There may be as much pedantry and waste of time in wrangling over the question to which of our nine hypothetical Minoan epochs a particular potsherd belongs, as in elaborating theories about the different usages of ἄν and οὖν. The shadow of the commentator, whatever may be his particular calling—textual criticism, grammar, excavation—should never be allowed (as it so often has been) to obscure and almost to obliterate the writing of genius. The true scholar values and uses all these aids and lights, each in its due proportion ; but the true scholar is rare.

Amidst all the digging and scratching and scraping that have been going on during the last twenty years on all sides of the Mediterranean, it is disappointing, though perhaps it ought not to be surprising, that so few of the lost literary treasures of the ancient world have been recovered. The caprice of chance, which has preserved so much, and left so much apparently to perish, still seems to mock our hopes. It is tempting to speculate which of the works that we know to have existed would, if rediscovered, be most warmly welcomed by the educated world. The lost Attic tragedies ? or the comedies of Menander ? or those discourses and dialogues of

Aristotle, which, if ancient tradition is credible, reveal him as the master of a readable and even an attractive style? or the *Philippica* of Theopompus, which, according to Wilamowitz von Moellendorff's[1] recent Oxford lecture, contained more than the special merits of Herodotus and Thucydides, and his equally remarkable *Meropis*, which was actually in existence in the ninth century. We would gladly exchange a little early Minoan pottery for some of these masterpieces—or indeed for some genuine product of the chisel of Phidias or Polyclitus. But it may be that these things are still only in hiding, to reward the patience or the good luck of some fortunate member of the indefatigable and undefeated fraternity of the spade.

In truth, the great writers of antiquity remain, as they have been and always will be, their own best interpreters. Archaeology has thrown, as it were from outside, new lights upon their environment, which have in not a few instances made real what seemed to be fantastic, and intelligible what was all but meaningless. But perhaps a still greater service has been rendered in our time to English scholarship by the wider knowledge and more comprehensive survey of ancient literature itself which is now required of any one who aspires to be a scholar. Thirty or forty years ago, at both Oxford and Cambridge,

---

[1] *Greek Historical Writings, etc.*, translated by Gilbert Murray. Oxford: Clarendon Press, 1908.

the so-called Classical authors were a select,
almost an aristocratic body. They were studied
with a minute and even meticulous care. I suppose there was not a sentence or even a line
in the *Ethics* or the *Republic*, every possible
interpretation of which was not as familiar to
the great Oxford coaches as are the traditional
openings in chess to a Lasker or a Tarrasch.
The well-regulated student was kept somewhat
rigorously within this carefully fenced domain.
If he showed vagrant, migratory tastes, which
tempted him to roam afield, he was warned against
the double danger of a too superficial knowledge
of his authors and a vitiated style. Intensive
cultivation of the writers of the Golden Age was
the rule of life. *Nocturna versate manu, versate
diurna*, was its motto. It is probable that very
few of us who were immersed in the great
Augustans ever read a line of Strabo, or of Diony-
sius of Halicarnassus, or of the anonymous author
of the treatise on the " Sublime "—though two
of them were certainly, and the third may
possibly, have been contemporary with Virgil
and Horace. There is, I am glad to say, a growing tendency to extend the range of classical
reading. There is no fear of the great masters
of style and literary charm being dethroned
from their seats of power. Homer, the Attic
dramatists, Herodotus, Thucydides, and Plato,
and, at Rome, Lucretius and Catullus, the

Augustan poets, Cicero, Livy, and Tacitus, will always maintain an undisputed ascendency. But, even though a man should put in peril the purity of his elegiacs and iambics, or of his Greek and Latin prose, his scholarship is one-sided and incomplete unless he makes himself at home in less familiar epochs and in fields that have been less assiduously tilled. The two fascinating books of Professor Dill show what a mine of interest, literary as well as historical, lies open for exploration in the later centuries of the Western Empire. And the *History of Classical Scholarship* by Dr. Sandys, the accomplished Public Orator of Cambridge, supplies a need from which we have all suffered, and for the first time provides English readers with a luminous and connected narrative, to use his own words, of " the accurate study of the language, literature, and art of Greece and Rome, and of all they had to teach us as to the nature and history of men." Dr. Sandys reminds us of what, possibly, even some members of the Association may have forgotten—the true origin of the term " Classical " which forms part of our title and which has given its name to a whole field of learning and research. In the *Noctes Atticae* (xix. 8. 15) Aulus Gellius describes a certain author as *classicus scriptor, non proletarius*, a metaphor which apparently goes back as far as the division of the Roman people into classes by Servius Tullius. A citizen in the first class was called *classicus*; those who made up the last and the lowest were *proletarii*. There are many authors, ancient as well as modern, who are more read than they deserve to be; for they belong irretrievably to the proletariat of literature. But I venture to think that in days gone by we have been a little too subservient to tradition and convention in refusing to admit the title of original and interesting writers to be ranked with the Classics.

Lastly, may I not say, without any disparagement of the great scholars of our youth, that what we call the Classics—whether as instrument of education or as field for research—have come to be treated with a larger outlook, in a more scientific spirit, with a quickened consciousness of their relations to other forms of knowledge and other departments of investigation. This is indeed a characteristic of the general intellectual movement of our time. It is more and more recognised that the many mansions which go to form the Palace of Knowledge and Truth open out into each other. There is no longer any question of mutual exclusion, still less of absorption or supersession. I was much struck with this in reading the brilliant address delivered this autumn to the assembled votaries of Natural Science by the President of the British Association. Mechanical theories and explanations no longer satisfy the well-equipped biologist and

I

botanist, who has to deal with the problem of living matter even in its most rudimentary forms. In like manner the facile and attractive simplicity of many of the theories which had crystallised almost into dogmas as to Greek origins, Greek religion, the order and development of Greek poetry, and as to a hundred other points, has had to yield to the sapping operations of the comparative method, and is found in the new setting of a larger scheme of knowledge to be hopelessly out of perspective. There is nothing more irksome to the natural man than to have the presuppositions on which he has lived rooted up and cast upon the rubbish heap. But this is the often unwelcome service which Science is always rendering to the world. Aristotle said long ago that the being that could live in isolation was either below or above humanity. There is no form of study—least of all the study of language and literature, which are the vesture of men's thoughts and emotions—that can afford to isolate itself without incurring the risks of pedantry and sterility.

Here is a work which is worthy of the co-operative efforts of this association of scholars. For the literature of the two great European races of the ancient world can never lose its supreme attraction, its incommunicable splendour; and of them it is true, in the famous words of Roger Bacon, *notitia linguarum est prima porta sapientiae.*

VI

THE ENGLISH BAR

VI

THE ENGLISH BAR [1]

MR. ATTORNEY-GENERAL AND GENTLEMEN OF THE BAR—You do not need to be assured that no compliment could be more grateful to me, or to any man who, like myself, has been for more than thirty years a member of the English Bar, than such a welcome as has been given to me to-night by the members of the great profession, among whom the laborious days of my life have been so largely spent. It enhances to me the value of that compliment that you should have selected as your mouthpiece my learned friend, Sir Edward Clarke. It has been my misfortune both in political and in professional life to be more often against than with Sir Edward Clarke; but whether with him or against him I have always felt—and which of us has not?—that there is no one among our contemporaries whom I should more heartily advise a young man entering the professional arena to look to as model, whether of temper, of method, of style, or of the

---

[1] Delivered at the Inner Temple Hall, July 10, 1908.

whole art of advocacy. Courage which, though always undaunted, never blusters ; persuasiveness which seems rather to win than to capture assent ; eloquence which never sacrifices light to heat,—those are qualities of which no man at the Bar in my time has been a more perfect and consummate exponent. Mr. Attorney, this is a gathering of the Bar, and of the Bar alone ; and almost for the first time (for it does not happen frequently in our lives) we are able to talk without turning our eyes, or directing our attention, either to the Bench above or to the Well below. To me I must confess that to speak anywhere in the region of the Temple without a tribunal, without a client, without a brief, and, I must add, without a fee, is an unfamiliar and in some ways a nerve-shaking experience. I can only wish that I were imbued for the moment with some portion of the magnificent *sang-froid* of that accomplished advocate Sir Richard Bethell, who is said —I daresay some of you know the legend—in the midst of a super-subtle argument, when harassed by the interlocutory irrelevance of a Chancery Judge, to have turned round to his unhappy junior, and to have exclaimed in an audible aside, " The damned fool has taken your point."

Well, gentlemen, as I am among old friends and brethren, I may, perhaps, be allowed for a moment—and only for a moment—to be egotistic and autobiographical. Let me, then, seize the opportunity—and I am glad to have it—of recalling the names and the memories of two illustrious lawyers to whom I feel myself always under special obligation. The first is my old master, Charles Bowen, afterwards one of the brightest ornaments of our Bench, in whose chambers not far from here, in Brick Court, I served my pupilage. I learnt, I hope, many things there, and amongst the other lessons which I learnt was one which every man who aspires to practise with success at the Bar in these days has to learn sooner or later, and that was the dangers, the multiform and manifold dangers, of an encounter with Danckwerts. Later on, after some pretty lean years, in which one used to welcome as an unexpected and grateful phenomenon a County Court brief, marked one guinea, and coming from a client whose time and method of payment were both nebulous and problematical, I had the singular good-fortune of securing the favour and help of a great man, my dear and revered friend, Lord James of Hereford. I owe to him a debt which he has never thought of exacting, and which I can never repay. May I add to those a third name—the name of one whom, I think, all the older men among us will agree with me in placing in the very first and highest rank of the advocates, either of our own or of any other time, Charles Russell? I was privileged, as Sir Edward Clarke has reminded me, to be associated with him as his junior in the greatest State trial of the Victorian era. We had as colleagues my noble friend the present Lord Chancellor, and a man of infinite humour and of unique lovableness, whose untimely death was to me and to all his friends an irreparable loss —the late Frank Lockwood. Mr. Attorney and gentlemen, those are memories which time can never efface. Sir Edward Clarke has referred to the fact that it is just about one hundred years since a practising member of the Bar was last Prime Minister of England. He was kind enough not to remind me that that predecessor came to a sudden and untimely end. *Absit omen!* But every age has its own peculiar dangers. It has been suggested to me by what Sir Edward Clarke has said, that in our school-days we all read of a certain legendary character, who seems to have tried to deal with a feminist movement somewhere in Thrace by euphonious generalities, and he, as a result, was torn to pieces by wild women. History, happily, does not always, or even often, repeat itself.

It is natural, perhaps, that on an occasion like this one should be tempted to reflect upon the relations in our history between politics and the law. The " gentlemen of the long robe," of the " *nisi prius* mind," have provided from time to time ample material for the cheap sarcasms of superficial and uninstructed politicians. Once, at any rate, and I think only once, in our history they were able to put these prejudices into practice, and the disastrous experiment was tried of a House of Commons from which all lawyers were excluded. What was the result? That notorious body, pilloried in our history as the *Parliamentum indoctum*, of which Lord Coke, not perhaps an altogether impartial judge, declares that the whole of its legislation was not worth twopence. Gentlemen, I make this claim, that there is no class or profession in our community which has done more — I will go further, I will say that there is none which has done as much—to define, to develop, and to defend the liberties of England. Sir Thomas More, Lord Coke himself, Selden, Somers, Camden, Romilly — those are but a few of the names selected almost at random from a long and illustrious roll. They were all bred in the common law of England, which is not a compendium of mechanical rules written in fixed and indelible characters, but a living organism, which has grown and moved in response to the larger and fuller development of the nation. The common law of England has been, still is, and will continue to be, both here and wherever English communities are found, at once the organ and the safeguard of English justice and English freedom.

There is another aspect of our meeting to-

night—a domestic rather than a public aspect—
with which you will allow me for a moment, and
in conclusion, to deal. This is, as Sir Edward
Clarke said, in many respects a unique gathering ;
and while I am more touched and grateful than
I can find any words to express for your fraternal
hospitality, I am not vain enough to interpret it
merely as a personal tribute to myself. I think
it has a much wider significance. As the Attorney-
General said, our life, by the very necessities of
our profession, is spent in constant and unceasing
conflict. We breathe every day an atmosphere
of eager, strenuous, unsparing controversy. Your
gathering to-night is surely characteristic of the
temper and of the traditions of the English
Bar. Here we are sitting round these tables in
friendship and in brotherhood, united in doing
honour to a member of our common profession
to whom fortune has been kind. Why is that ?
The reason, to those of us who know the real
spirit of the Bar, is plain, and it is this. The
arduous struggle, the blows given and received,
the exultation of victory, the sting of defeat,
which are our daily experience, far from breeding
division and ill-will, only bind us more closely
together by the ties of a comradeship for which
you would look in vain in any other arena of the
ambitions and the rivalries of men. Gentlemen,
I thank you with all my heart for one of the
greatest honours of my life.

VII

AD PORTAS

.

VII

AD PORTAS [1]

SALUTATIONI vestrae, Wiccamici, cum propter
singularem erga nos benevolentiam acceptissimae,
tum facundia perpolita haud minus admirandae,
ita respondere conabor ut, quamvis diutius a
Musis remotus, ad tantum orationis nitorem non
facile perveniam, amicitia tamen non desim.
Nullam enim sententiam, confiteor, Aulae Praefecte, a te mihi gratius excidisse quam illud " non
omnino externus ac peregrinus accedis." Nam,
si non Wiccamicum, tamen quasi Wiccamicum
adoptivum, ad egregiam illam Wiccamicorum
sodalitatem me benignius adscivisti. Immo for-
sitan si ut Romae, ita hic, jus trium liberorum
obtinere soleat, vestrae haud immerito societati
adrogatus esse videar: qui huic Collegio quat-
tuor jam dederim filios, quintum mox daturus, si
ad plenam civitatem non aliter licet aspirare.

Nimirum mihi perjucundum esse facile credetis,
publicarum onere curarum diem licet unum re-

¹ Reply to an Address of Welcome from the Prefect of Hall,
Winchester College, July 27, 1909.

posito, fumo strepituque urbis procul relicto, e tanta rerum vertigine ad hanc vestram Academiam, Musis tamdiu consecratam, confugere, animum atque oculos inter serenas amoenitates vestras recreare. Inter quas vir praeclarissimus,[1] Collega mihi valde dilectus, vires illas ingenii cum solidi tum sobrii et, ut ita dicam, admodum Wiccamici, otio puer operosiore corroboravit. Quodsi, Aulae Praefecte, ut nuper intellexi, non modo animi refectionem sed corporis etiam incolumitatem polliceri potes, et Erinyas istas licebit πορρῶθεν ἀσπάζεσθαι, has sedes unice securus ingrediar.

[1] Sir Edward Grey.

VIII

THE ENGLISH BIBLE

VIII

THE ENGLISH BIBLE [1]

WHAT I am about to say I speak as a layman who claims his allotted share in the most universally prized possession in the common heritage of the English-speaking world. Three centuries, as you have been reminded, have passed since, after nearly seven years employed in research, in translation, in revision, and in printing, our Authorised Version of the Bible was first given to the world. It is worth while to recall that those seven years, during which the six companies of translators were quietly engaged upon their task, were in other fields the most remarkable and fruitful in the annals of English literature. The great Queen herself was dead, but the two supreme geniuses of what we call the Elizabethan era were still in the meridian and plenitude of their powers. In 1605, the year after the Hampton Court Conference, Francis Bacon

K

published his *Advancement of Learning*. Between 1604 and 1610 Shakespeare produced in succession his tragedies, *Othello*, *Macbeth*, and *King Lear*, and the year 1611—the year of the Authorised Version—was the year in which, as we believe, he wrote *The Tempest*, and with it, in Prospero's phrase, finally broke his magician's wand. But in the meantime, in 1608, here in London, there had been seen the birth of perhaps the only English writer who was worthy to take up that great succession—the "God-gifted organ voice of England," John Milton. Nor should it be forgotten that we had then among us, born ten years earlier, and still "muing his mighty youth," one Oliver Cromwell.

Sir, it was an age of giants in thought, in writing, and in action; and yet, as the Archbishop has reminded us, our Authorised Version, which was brought to birth in this heroic atmosphere, was the joint product of what in these days we call a syndicate of some fifty men, the names of very few of whom are known to any but the curious student of the bypaths of history. From that point of view the English Bible may be regarded as standing alone among the masterpieces of literature.

But, as we have been already told, we ought, when we are rendering gratitude to those to whom we owe this unique treasure, to trace the stream to its fountain-head. Great and incom-

parable as were the services rendered by the
translators in the time of James I., our Bible in
its most essential and characteristic features is
not of Elizabethan, still less is it of Jacobean
authorship. The early translations of the disciples of Wycliffe, never perhaps with a wide
circulation, not even printed by Caxton himself,
were already archaic, and probably obsolete, when
the Renaissance reached England at the end of
the fifteenth century. Those versions seem to
have been unknown to the two great men to
whom, more than to any one else, we owe our
English Bible — William Tyndale and Miles
Coverdale. It is a singular fact that it was in
the reign of Henry VIII., an otherwise relatively
sterile era in our language and literature, that
these two men of genius, with their contemporary
Cranmer, created the literary form, with its
matchless cadences and its sublime simplicity,
which is inseparably associated in the mind and
the thought of all English-speaking people with
the history of the Old Testament, with the
poetry of the Psalmists and the Prophets, with
the narratives of the Incarnation, with the
message of the Apostles and the Evangelists, and
with all the infinitely varied appeals of devotion,
praise, and prayer.

There is a celebrated retort reported to
have been made to an obscurantist critic by
Tyndale himself—Tyndale, confessor and martyr,

in the greatest campaign ever waged by the soldiers of freedom against the forces of intellectual and spiritual tyranny—a celebrated retort in which he said, "If God spare my life, ere many years I will cause a boy that driveth the plough to know more of the Scriptures than thou dost." Never has what looked like a hazardous prediction, if not a vainglorious boast, been more amply or richly fulfilled. To the common people of England, when Tyndale began to translate the New Testament, the Bible was a collection of oracles in a dead language. Their interpretation was the monopoly of a sacerdotal caste. Even Sir Thomas More himself thought that an English translation should not be hazarded except with a safeguard, the safeguard that all the copies should be entrusted to the Bishops, and doled out at their discretion only to such as the Bishops should perceive to be "honest, sad, and virtuous." The circulation of the Bible in English, first surreptitiously, then with the connivance, and at last with the open approval, of the State, as Tyndale's and Coverdale's translations, the Great Bible, the Bishops' Bible, the Geneva Bible, finally our Authorised Version—the circulation of the Bible in English was, in my judgment, in a far truer sense than the legislation of Henry and Elizabeth the moving force of the Reformation.

It delivered our people from a yoke to which

they will never again submit. It opened to one and all, small and great, poor and rich, learned and ignorant, the treasure-house of the Divine wisdom. It gave to each, in the daily round of labour and care, as well as in the supreme and testing moments of life, an equal and unstinted share in the teachings which inspire, the consolations which soothe, the faith which can move mountains, the hope which endures to the end.

And if the English Bible has been to the English people an instrument of inspiration, has not it also been, and ought it not increasingly to be, the symbol and safeguard of unity? There are gathered here to-night on this platform and in this hall the representatives of many Churches and communities. He, let me add, must be a very superficial student of history who thinks that you can summarily account for the divisions of Christendom as the product merely of misunderstanding and confusion, of want of perspective, or of petty jealousies and rivalries. But all of us, by whatever ecclesiastical label we are designated, all of us have in the English Bible a common possession, a common inheritance, a common storehouse and reservoir of religious thought and teaching. This tercentenary will not have been celebrated in vain if it brings home to us with a new emphasis the truth that, while there are diversities of operation, there is one and the same spirit—the spirit whose message we have all of us read in the same familiar and yet venerable language from the first moment that we were able to speak.

As I have implied more than once, the English Bible belongs not only to the subjects of the King but to the whole English-speaking world. We are delighted, as you, my lord, have already said, to welcome on the platform my distinguished friend, the American Ambassador. His presence reminds us that across the seas, mainly of our own kindred, though owning a different allegiance, there has grown up, since the date of the Authorised Version, a mighty nation, who claim with us a share in what is to us and to them a common possession. It was John Robinson, as many of you will remember, the Pastor of the Pilgrim Fathers, who, on the eve of their departure, declared in a memorable sentence that " the Lord has more truths yet to bring forth out of His Holy Word."

One of the truths which we have slowly realised, and which is now firmly rooted, as I believe, in the faith of all Christian men and women on both sides of the Atlantic, is that war between English-speaking peoples would not only be a crime against civilisation, but an unforgivable breach of those new commandments that are enshrined and consecrated in the New Testament, on which both nations have been bred. There surely could not be a worthier, a more appropriate, a more splendid monument of this tercentenary year, than that it should witness the sealing of a solemn pact between us which would put an end once and for all to the hideous, the unthinkable possibilities of fratricidal strife.

IX

EDINBURGH

IX

EDINBURGH [1]

I ESTEEM it a high honour to be allowed to sub-
scribe my name to the burgess roll of the capital
city of Scotland. Though not a Scotsman by
birth, I am, as the Lord Provost has already
said, very near being senior among the Scottish
representatives at Westminster. When I first
invaded Scotland, five-and-twenty years ago, a
ferry - boat conveyed me and my carpet - bag
across the turbulent and treacherous waters of
the Forth to the adjacent Kingdom of Fife,
which has been my political home ever since.

Since those days a great bridge has made communication between Fife and the Lothians more
easy and more frequent. It remains true, as it
was then and as it will continue to be, that there
is no part of Scotland, however remote in distance
and however independent in spirit, that does not
recognise that the centre and mainspring of our
national life is to be found in this great historic

[1] Speech delivered at Edinburgh on receiving the Freedom of
the City, December 20, 1910.

capital. It would be late in the day, even if it were becoming for your youngest burgess, to attempt to sound the praises of this ancient and famous city; to speak of the unsurpassed beauty of its situation and surroundings; of the stirring and moving scenes of which century after century it has been the theatre; of the great men that it has bred and nourished and taught and sheltered, the " hands that penned and tongues that uttered wisdom "; the poets, the orators, the philosophers, the statesmen, the lawyers, the divines, and —most illustrious of them all—that supreme creative imagination which stands second only to Shakespeare in our literature. One is sometimes tempted to think that one of the least desirable results of the gigantic development in the nineteenth century of the means of communication has been its tendency to drain away from the centres of our local life their separateness and their individuality. Many of our ancient English towns have felt, and to some extent suffered from, the change. Even here, although in a much lesser degree, you have not altogether escaped the levelling influence of East and West Coast services by night and by day. We shall, I suppose, never see here again the same concentration and isolation—if I may use the phrase —of social and literary interests as was to be found in the Edinburgh of Robertson, of Mackenzie, of Dugald Stewart, and of Walter Scott.

But for all that, Edinburgh, it may be said without flattery or exaggeration, maintains in a large measure a life and a savour of its own. No one who knows her at all can ever imagine while he is here that he is anywhere else. The modern world with its steam-roller methods, its levelling of inequalities, its lopping of excrescences, its rounding of angles and blunting of edges, all of them in due place and season healthful and even necessary processes, tends inevitably and increasingly towards uniformity, sameness, monotony. Let us do all we can, both in our children and in our cities, to keep fresh and potent the saving salt of individuality.

But the Edinburgh of to-day is not content to live on the memories of its past. She is not content even — strong though the temptation must sometimes be—to gaze complacently as in a looking-glass on the reflection of those gifts and graces with which she is so richly endowed, and which have been denied to more commonplace towns. No; she carries on an active, a progressive municipal life, and in no department, I am glad to say, more conspicuously or more fruitfully than in that of education in all its branches. I need say nothing of the sustained vigour and undimmed fame of your great University and its medical school. Nor is it necessary to enlarge upon the efficiency of your elementary schools, from each of which I am delighted to hear there are children present in this hall to-day. I will only note in passing, and with sincere gratification, the growing attention which is being paid to those physical conditions—proper feeding, vigilant medical supervision—without due regard to which the best intellectual training is a futile mockery. But here in Edinburgh the most striking developments have been in other parts of the educational field. I refer particularly to your training college for teachers, the college of art, the agricultural college, the school for domestic economy, and last, but by no means least, the more than encouraging measure of success which is attending your continuation classes for pupils who have left school and for adults. Here, both in legislation and in administration, we in Scotland may claim to be well ahead of our own fellow-subjects on the other side of the Border. I said some weeks ago in Glasgow, when I had the honour of receiving the freedom of that great city, that one of the most tragic sights in our town life is that of the boy sitting at the tail-end of a van reading some trashy story; forgetting every day more and more of what he was taught at school; receiving no training of any kind for any permanent calling; rapidly graduating, as soon as his present precarious short-lived occupation comes to an end, for a place in the ranks of the unemployable. For years past this has been the darkest blot and the most fatal gap in our educational system. Edinburgh, in my judgment at any rate, can perform no greater services to the nation than by grappling with this evil, and thereby showing to the other great communities of the country the way towards the drastic and curative treatment of one of the most fertile causes of poverty and crime.

A large part of my life, practically the whole of it that is known to my fellow-citizens, has been spent in contention and in public controversy. Nor am I sanguine enough to hope that I am at this moment at the opening of a new chapter which is to tell of nothing but peace, unanimity, and repose. There are many members of your corporation and civic roll who have not always agreed with me in the past, and possibly may not find it easy always to agree with me in the future. But, following the generous traditions of our public life, all alike have joined in this signal and most welcome and touching tribute to one who, sometimes in arduous circumstances, has tried to do his duty and serve the State. I thank you with a full heart, and I beg you to believe that there is no honour which, after sitting as I have twenty-five years as a Scottish representative at Westminster, could be more grateful to me than that I should be thought worthy of the freedom of the City of Edinburgh.

X

THE ROYAL SOCIETY

X

THE ROYAL SOCIETY[1]

THE 250th anniversary of the Royal Society is appropriately commemorated in this Guildhall. For " The Royal Society of London for the Improving of Natural Knowledge," to give it its original title, though it has become eminently a national institution, has at the same time peculiarly close associations with the City of London. In the first charter, which, I think, was signed 250 years ago yesterday, permission was given to the Society to " assemble in a college or other public place or hall within our City of London, or in any other convenient place within ten miles of the same." When the Universities were engrossed in the din of the Civil War, " to the neglect," as a contemporary writer says, " of academical studies," science and philosophy took refuge in the comparative peace and tranquillity which the streets of the City of London could then afford. The troubled reign of Charles I.

[1] Speech delivered at the Celebration of the 250th Anniversary at the Guildhall, July 16, 1912.

gathered to London—I again quote contemporary words—" divers worthy persons inquisitive into natural philosophy and other parts of human learning," men whose imagination and enthusiasm had been fired by the " New Philosophy " then recently propounded. In the later days of the Commonwealth their meetings were held for a time in my own University of Oxford at Wadham College, of which I am glad to see the Warden here to-night ; and after the Restoration they found their headquarters within a few hundred yards of this hall at Old Gresham College, which was the birthplace and cradle, and for some time the regular place of meeting, of the Royal Society.

The record of the Society begins, I think justly, with a tribute to the influence of Francis Bacon, whose fertile mind not only conceived the advantages of a college co-operating in the investigation of natural philosophy, but also in his *New Atlantis* outlined a practical plan for its foundation. As Mr. Balfour said recently, Bacon's great service to science was that " he created the atmosphere in which scientific dis-covery flourishes." From the publication of the *Novum Organum* we may trace a steady and an ever-increasing interest in the experimental sciences, and Bacon's scheme finally found realisa-tion in the incorporation of the Royal Society. Its proud motto, " Nullius in Verba," reproduces the true spirit of what is best in Bacon's teaching.

But if the Society can trace its spiritual ancestry to Francis Bacon, the actual figure of the pious founder is to be discovered in a very different quarter. Strange as it may seem, the Royal Society is to-day the most vital, if not the most characteristic, monument of King Charles II. Whether the interest in anatomy displayed, as your annals show, by the Society in its earliest years was due to the proclivities of its Royal patron, I do not know; but certain it is that Charles II. not only founded the Society, but he took an active interest in its proceedings and frequently asked for its advice. And he could not have found a body more representative of the best and the widest culture of his time.

When one looks over the list of the original Fellows, what strikes one is the width and the universality of the interests represented. Science could not then, whatever may be the case now, be charged with being the preserve of specialised studies. With Robert Boyle, John Wilkins, Robert Hooke—scientific men, in our somewhat narrow use of the term—there come Sir Christopher Wren, that early prodigy, as he is called, of universal science, astronomer, physicist, physiologist, as well as our greatest architect, perhaps the most versatile intelligence that Europe has seen since Leonardo da Vinci; Cowley and Dryden, Denham and Waller, better known to posterity as poets than philosophers; Evelyn,

Aubrey, Petty, and a host of others, whose names recall the spiritual and intellectual wealth of an epoch which we are wont too often to decry. In the same roll with John Dryden is one of the chief victims of his satire, George Villiers, Duke of Buckingham, who amid his various qualifications for the chief office of State was, as we know, " chemist, fiddler, statesman, and buffoon." And I see from your records that history tells us that when this, perhaps the most original of the original Fellows of the Royal Society, was committed to the Tower, a special laboratory was fitted up for him there in order that he might practise chemistry ; and according to Bishop Burnet, he was " nearly " successful in discovering the philosopher's stone—an illustration which suggests that some people might be more profitably employed at present than either at Westminster or Whitehall.

The bulk, however, of the original Fellows of the Royal Society appear to have been, in the words of your first historian, Bishop Sprat, " gentlemen, free and unconfined." The Society to this day numbers among its Fellows those who, like myself, have no claim to take any part but that of spectators in the pursuit of the natural sciences, and who belong, like our predecessors in the reign of Charles II., so far as this branch of activity is concerned, to the category of the unemployed. In the genial diary of Samuel

Pepys, himself a Fellow, and, indeed, at one time, I think, President of the Society, there are entries that throw light on its early activities, which, in those days, whatever may be the case now, were much given to experiment. On one occasion he records meeting in a tavern " a man, a little frantic, whom the College hath hired for 20 shillings to have some of the blood of a sheep let into his body, and it is to be done on Saturday next." From a later entry it appears that " the gentleman found himself much better since, and as a new man, and will have it done again, but," adds the diarist, " he is a little cracked." But if we are too ready to laugh at these early extravagances of experimental science, it is as well also to remember that it was under the auspices of Pepys that Newton's *Principia* was produced.

I will not linger over these reminiscences of the early days of the Society. The foundation so fairly started has had a continuous career of success and illustrious work. It has not escaped its share of criticism and ridicule; but it has justified itself by its deeds. The position which makes the letters F.R.S. one of the proudest additions which an Englishman can make to his name has been won by the sheer weight of meritorious work.

The Society has not, I think, at any time had any direct financial assistance from the Government. For this the Government may be criticised ; but I venture to think the Society is to be congratulated. It is not well that Science should be a mendicant for State endowment. I do not forget the annual grants for scientific research which are administered by the Society ; but their administration is not a benefit conferred on the Society by the State, but a service rendered to the State by the Society.

It would not be possible for any one to traverse in a few moments the history of the Society, or to chronicle the achievements of its Fellows, without at the same time traversing and chronicling the history of English science itself. There is hardly a year when your roll has not been enriched by a name to which not only we, as Englishmen, but the whole world is indebted for a share in the slow but steady subjection of Nature to the intelligence of man—that process which is best described in Bacon's immortal words : *Natura non nisi parendo vincitur.* If we recall the names of Isaac Newton, who was, I think, for a quarter of a century President of the Society, of Locke, Flamsteed and Halley, Sir Hans Sloane, Adam Smith, Woolaston and Watt, Davy and Faraday, Pringle and Young, or, closer to our own time, Darwin, Huxley, Hooker, Herschel, Huggins, Sir Michael Foster, Lord Kelvin, and one whose loss we lamented only a few months ago, perhaps the greatest benefactor in our time of the human race, Lord Lister—the roll contains the names of England's worthiest children in the wide field of work which is comprised in the original project of this foundation. The Royal Society which honoured them, and was honoured by them, is remembered when we remember them one and all. It has grown with the growth of England ; it has advanced with the advance of science ; and it stands now, after 250 years, firmly established in the confidence of the nation and the respect of the world, still faithful, still fruitful in the cause of human progress and human enlightenment.

XI

THE RUBÁIYÁT OF OMAR KHAYYÁM

XI

THE RUBÁIYÁT OF OMAR KHAYYÁM[1]

I ESTEEM it a high honour, for which I return you my heartfelt thanks, to have been invited here to-night as the guest of your Club. There are few greater benefactors of the species than the man who discovers a new bond of human companionship and a fresh excuse for social intercourse. If that be true, as I believe it is, the founders of this club are entitled to a special measure of gratitude. For they have not only hit upon a hitherto untried expedient for bringing men together to eat and drink and talk, but they have, at the same time, invented a most admirable test—if I may, without irreverence, borrow a phrase from the terminology of the Presbyterian Church — for " fencing the tables " against the intrusion of pedants, Philistines, and bores. I do not say that faith in our Omar Khayyám, and FitzGerald as his prophet, is the narrow road by which alone a man may find his way to literary and social salvation. Apart from other

---

[1] Delivered to the Omar Khayyám Club, April 27, 1898.

reasons which might be adduced, it is enough for
us here to say that such intolerance ought to be
impossible to the followers of a poet who, in his
most dogmatic mood, will not go farther than
to concede that

> A hair perhaps divides the False and True;

and who is uttering his settled judgment of men's
differences, whether of taste, opinion, or creed,
when he extols

> The Grape that can with Logic absolute,
> The Two-and-Seventy jarring Sects confute.

But this, at least, we may assert with confidence,
that no man, who has breathed the true spirit
of our poet and his great interpreter, can be any
longer a slave to the conventions which sterilise
and devastate such large areas of social intercourse. To admire and delight in Omar, as he
is presented to us by FitzGerald, is one of those
subtle bonds of sympathy which are constantly
creating new ties of kinship, and new groups of
association, among men who are moved by the
art which belongs not to one age or country
but to all.

You have had many appreciations of Omar
from far more capable hands than mine. Nor
has he escaped faithful treatment from the critics,
who shake their sorrowful heads over his manifold
lapses from the path of orthodox belief and
correct conduct. A poet who avows that he
sampled and rejected the various beliefs which

were on exhibition in the market of his day—
who tells us that he

evermore
Came out by the same Door where in I went—

bears a perilous resemblance to the Agnostic
whom some of us have met. The preacher who
exhorts his followers to abandon the wearing
pursuit of the secret of life; to sit down and fill
their cups with the " old familiar juice " ; and
not to " heed the rumble of a distant drum," is
not very far from the " sty of Epicurus." Why
is it that, from the moment the genius of Fitz-
Gerald made him known to all who speak the
English language, he has taken rank with the
immortals whom no change of taste or fashion
can dethrone ? I do not pretend to give a full
answer to the question, but there are one or two
considerations which are obvious. First, as regards form, apart from the strange fascination
of the metre, there is within a narrow compass,
in point of actual bulk, a wholeness and com-
pleteness in Omar which belongs only to the
highest art. You remember Heine's apology for
the fragmentary character of his " Atta Troll."
It must be content, he says in the preface, to
remain unfinished, like so many of the great
works of German genius—Cologne Cathedral,
the God of Schelling, and the Prussian Constitu-
tion. There is nothing in Omar's work that
could be added to or taken from it without

injuring its perfection. Then, as regards sub-
stance, where else in literature has the littleness of
man, contrasted with the baffling infinitude of his
environment, and the resulting duty of serenity
and acquiescence, been more brilliantly painted
or more powerfully enforced ? The million
bubbles that the Eternal Saki pours from his
bowl; the clay which lies passive under the thump-
ing of the Potter; the ball that is thrown hither
and thither about the field; the helpless pawns
that the great Player moves into impossible
positions with an inscrutable purpose; the end-
less procession of empty pageantries; the sultans
and heroes who, with all their pomp and pride,
are after all but passing inmates of this " batter'd
caravanserai "—such is the crowd of vivid and
moving images which Omar's panorama presents
to us. As we gaze upon it the individual withers;
the great men, who seemed to the intoxicated
vision of their own time to be the dominating
forces of the world, are seen to be but the flicker-
ing motes in the sunbeam : the crest raised by
a gust of wind upon the rising and falling wave.

> The Wine of Life keeps oozing drop by drop,
> The Leaves of Life keep falling one by one.

These, if I understand them aright, are the
thoughts and pictures with which Omar and
FitzGerald have permanently enriched the poetry
of the world.

XII

BENJAMIN JOWETT

XII

BENJAMIN JOWETT[1]

I HAVE one claim to speak to this Resolution which is not shared by either of the noble Lords who have addressed you. It is that I am an old Balliol man, and, like all Balliol men, I should feel that any tribute to the memory of our late Master was not complete if it did not include an expression, however inadequate, of the gratitude and affection of the great College to which the best energies of his life were given. Both the country and the University of Oxford are the poorer by his death. England has lost in him a man of letters, who perhaps did more than any one to unlock to English readers the treasure-house of ancient literature. The University, represented to-day in this place by one who has the best title to speak in its name, recognises in him not only the great Professor and the great Vice-Chancellor, but, if I may say so, the last survivor of our heroic age. But

[1] Delivered at the Meeting at the University of London, December 2, 1893, "To consider the forms which could be most appropriately given to Memorials to the late Master of Balliol."

those of us who belong, as the Speaker and I do,
to Balliol, feel a more personal sense of loss.
It is as difficult for us to think of our College
without the Master as it would have been to
think of the Master without the College.   For the
best part of fifty years their lives have been
closely entwined, and I am not guilty of exaggeration if I say that, during the greater part of that
time, his character and his influence, more than
any other single force, have been the thread
which has connected, unbroken, the continuous
identity of the College, and bound together
successive generations of Balliol men.   That
thread, worn out by ceaseless service, has at last
snapped.   It is difficult, as Lord Salisbury has
said, perhaps it is impossible, to define, or even
to explain, the subtle power of his personality.
He had none of the vulgar marks of a successful
leader either of thought or action.   He founded
no school ; nor was he the author or the apostle
of any system, constructive or even critical.   In
a sense it is true that he left behind him no
disciples ; and to those who think that no man
can stamp his impress upon his generation unless
he is either a dogmatist or a partisan, his career
will be a constant puzzle.   But to us who knew
him and saw him in the daily life of the College,
the secret of his power is no mystery.   We cannot
hope to see again the counterpart of that refined
and fastidious mind, in whose presence intellectual

lethargy was stirred into life, and intellectual pretentiousness sank into abashed silence. Still less can we hope to see a character such as his; the union of worldly sagacity with the most transparent simplicity of nature; an intelligence keen and unsleeping, but entirely detached, and absorbed in the fortunes of a great institution and its members. Upon his generosity no call could be too heavy; with his delicate kindliness he was ever ready to give the best hours of either the day or the night to help and to advise the humblest of those who appealed to him for aid. These are the qualities, or some of the qualities, which were the secret of his personality, and which now are buried in his grave. No man of our time, and few men of any time, can be more truly said to have lived for the sake of his work. Of that work Balliol College was from the beginning, and remained to the end, the centre and the inspiration. He has gone. We who remain, and who owe him so much, may be sure of this— that there is no tribute which would have been more welcome to him, and there is no memorial which can more fittingly perpetuate his name, than one which, while it expresses the gratitude and the admiration of Englishmen of every class and creed, will provide for the continuance of his work within the walls of the College where he lived, and which he served, all the days of his life.

XIII

SIR HENRY CAMPBELL-BANNERMAN

XIII

SIR HENRY CAMPBELL-BANNERMAN [1]

MR. SPEAKER—Many of us, sir, have come here
fresh from the service in Westminster Abbey,
where, amidst the monuments and memories of
great men, the nation took its last farewell of
all that was mortal in our late Prime Minister.
But, sir, there is not a man whom I am addressing
now who does not feel that our tribute to the dead
would be incomplete if this House, of which, by
seniority, he was the father, and which for many
years he led, were not to offer to his memory to-day
its own special mark of reverence and affection.
I shall therefore propose, before I sit down, that
we should lay aside for to-day the urgent business which has brought us together, and that the
House do at once adjourn until to-morrow.

It is within a few months of forty years since
Sir Henry Campbell-Bannerman took his seat
in this Chamber. Mr. Gladstone had just entered
upon his first Premiership in the plenitude of
his powers and of his authority. A new House,

[1] Speech delivered in the House of Commons, April 27, 1908.

elected upon an extended suffrage, had brought
to Westminster new men, new ideas; as some
thought, a new era.   Among the newcomers
there were probably few, judged by the superficial tests which are commonly applied, who
seemed less obviously destined than Mr. Campbell, as he then was, to fill the position he ulti-
mately reached.   There have been men who, in
the cruel phrase of the ancient historian, were
universally judged to be fit for the highest place
only until they attained and held it.   Our late
Prime Minister belonged to that rarer class whose
fitness for such a place, until they had attained
and held it, was never adequately understood.
It is true that he reached office much earlier in
his Parliamentary career than is the case with
most politicians.   In successive Governments, at
the War Office, at the Admiralty, at the Irish
Office, and at the War Office again, he rendered
devoted and admirable service to the State.   It
is no secret, and it is sufficient proof that he himself had no ambition for leadership, that, when
he was for the second time a Cabinet Minister,
he aspired, sir, to be seated in your chair.   But
though he had too modest an estimate of himself
to desire, and still less to seek, the first place in
the State, it fell to him, after years of much storm
and stress, by a title which no one disputed; and
he filled it with an ever-growing recognition in
all quarters of his unique qualifications.

What was the secret of the hold, which in these later days he unquestionably had, on the admiration and affection of men of all parties and men of all creeds ?   If, as I think was the case, he was one of those men who require to be fully known to be justly measured, may I say that the more we knew him, both followers and opponents, the more we became aware that on the moral as on the intellectual side he had endowments, rare in themselves, still rarer in their combination ? For example, he was singularly sensitive to human suffering and wrong-doing; delicate and even tender in his sympathies; always disposed to despise victories won in any sphere by mere brute force; an almost passionate lover of peace ; and yet we have not seen in our time a man of greater courage—courage not of a defiant and aggressive type, but calm, patient, persistent, indomitable.

Let me, sir, recall another apparent contrast in his nature. In politics I think he may be fairly described as an idealist in aim, and an optimist by temperament. Great causes appealed to him. He was not ashamed, even on the verge of old age, to see visions and to dream dreams. He had no misgivings as to the future of democracy ; he had a single-minded and unquenchable faith in the unceasing progress and the growing unity of mankind ; none the less, in the selection of men for the daily work of tilling the political field, in the choice of this man or that for some particular task, he showed not only that practical shrewdness which came to him from his Scottish ancestors, but a touch of the discernment and insight of a cultured citizen of the world.   In truth, Mr. Speaker, that which gave him the authority and affection, which, taken together, no one among his contemporaries enjoyed in an equal measure, was not one quality more than another, or any union of them : it was the man himself.   He never put himself forward, yet no one had greater tenacity of purpose ; he was the least cynical of mankind, but no one had a keener eye for the humours and ironies of the political situation.   He was a strenuous and uncompromising fighter, a strong party man, but he harboured no resentment. He was generous to a fault in appreciation of the work of others, whether friends or foes.   He met both good and evil fortune with the same un-clouded brow, the same unruffled temper, the same unshakable confidence in the justice and righteousness of his cause.   Sir Henry Campbell-Bannerman had hardly attained the highest place, and made himself fully known, when a domestic trial, the saddest that can come to any of us, darkened his days, and dealt what proved to be a mortal blow to his heart.   But he never for a moment shirked his duty to the State ; he laboured on—we here have seen it at close quarters — he laboured on under strain and anxiety; and, under a maiming sense of a loss that was ever fresh, he was always ready to respond to every public demand. And, sir, as we knew him here, so after he was stricken down in the midst of his work, a martyr, if ever there was one, to conscience and duty, so he continued to the end.

I can never forget the last time that I was privileged to see him, almost on the eve of his resignation. His mind was clear; his interest in the affairs of the country and of this House was undimmed; his talk was still lighted up by flashes of that homely, mellow wisdom peculiarly his own. Still more to be remembered are his serene patience, his untroubled equanimity, and the quiet trust with which during these long, weary days he awaited the call which he knew was soon to come. He has gone to his rest, and to-day in this House, of which he was the senior and the most honoured member, we may call a truce in the strife of parties, while we together remember our common loss, and pay our united homage to a gracious and cherished memory.

> How happy is he born or taught,
>   That serveth not another's will;
> Whose armour is his honest thought,
>   And simple truth his utmost skill!
> .   .   .   .   .   .
> This man is freed from servile bands
>   Of hope to rise, or fear to fall;
> Lord of himself, though not of lands;
>   And, having nothing, yet hath all.

XIV

KING EDWARD VII

XIV

KING EDWARD VII [1]

I FIND it my duty to make two Motions to the House. Though in point of form they will no doubt be put separately from the Chair, I think it right to read them both at once, and I shall confine what I have to say in support of both, in accordance with precedent, within the compass of a single speech. The first Motion is as follows :

That a humble Address be presented to His Majesty to assure His Majesty of the heartiest sympathy of this House in the grievous affliction and loss by the death of the late King, His Majesty's father, of blessed and glorious memory :

That we shall ever remember with grateful affection the zeal and success with which our late Sovereign laboured to consolidate the peace and concord of the world, to aid every merciful endeavour for the alleviation of human suffering, and to unite in justice and freedom all races and classes of his subjects with his Imperial Throne :

To offer His Majesty our loyal congratulations upon his auspicious accession :

To assure His Majesty of our devotion to his Royal person, and of our sure conviction that his reign will,

---

[1] Speech delivered in the House of Commons, May 11, 1910.

under the favour of Divine Providence, be distinguished by unswerving efforts to promote the virtue, prosperity, and contentment of the realm, and to guard the rights and liberties of His Majesty's faithful people.

The second Motion will be to the following effect :

That a message of condolence be sent to Her Majesty the Queen-Mother to assure Her Majesty of the deep and warm sympathy which this House feels for Her Majesty in this melancholy time of sorrow and irreparable loss ; and that this · House and the nation will ever preserve towards Her Majesty the sentiments of unalterable reverence and affection.

Mr. Deputy-Speaker, the late King, who has been suddenly taken from us, had at the time of his death not yet completed the tenth year of his reign. Those years were crowded with moving and stirring events, abroad, in the Empire, and here at home. In our relations with foreign countries they have been years of growing friendships, of new understandings, of stronger and surer safeguards for the peace of mankind. Within the Empire during the same time the sense of interdependence, the consciousness of common interests and common risks, the ever-tightening bonds of corporate unity, have been developed and vivified as they had never been before. Here at home, as though it were by way of contrast, controversial issues of the gravest kind—economic, social, constitutional—have ripened into a rapid maturity. In all these multiform manifestations of our national and Imperial life, history will assign a part of singular dignity and authority to the great Ruler whom we have lost.

In external affairs his powerful personal influence was steadily and zealously directed to the avoidance not only of war, but of the causes and pretexts of war, and he well earned the title by which he will always be remembered, " The Peacemaker of the World."

Within the boundaries of his own Empire, by his intimate knowledge of its component parts; by his broad and elastic sympathy, not only with the ambitions and the aspirations, but with the sufferings and the hardships of his people; by his ready response to any and every appeal, whether to the sense of justice or to the spirit of compassion; he won a degree of loyalty, affection, and confidence which few Sovereigns have ever enjoyed.

At home we all recognise that above the din and the dust of our hard-fought controversies, detached from party, attached only to the common interest, we had in him an arbiter, ripe in experience, judicial in temper, at once a reverent worshipper of our traditions, and a watchful guardian of our constitutional liberties.

One is tempted, indeed constrained, on such an occasion as this to ask what were the qualities which enabled a man called comparatively late

N 1

in life to new duties of unexampled complexity—
what were the qualities which in practice proved
him so admirably fitted to the task, and have
given him an enduring and illustrious record
among the rulers and governors of the nations.
I should be disposed to put first what sounds
a commonplace, but in its persistent and unfailing exercise is one of the rarest of virtues,
his strong, abiding, dominating sense of public
duty.   King Edward, be it remembered, was a
man of many and varied interests.   He was a
sportsman in the best sense, an ardent and
discriminating patron of the Arts.   He was as
well equipped as any man of his time for the
give-and-take of social intercourse ;   wholly free
from the prejudices and narrowing rules of caste ;
at home in all companies ;   an enfranchised
citizen of the world.   To such a man, endowed
as he was by nature, placed where he was by
fortune and by circumstance, there was open,
if he had chosen to enter it, an unlimited field
for self-indulgence.   But, sir, as every one will
acknowledge who was brought into daily contact
with him in the sphere of affairs, his duty to the
State always came first.   In this great business
community there was no better man of business ;
no man by whom the humdrum obligations—
punctuality, method, preciseness, and economy
of time and speech—were more keenly recognised
or more severely practised.   I speak with the

privilege of close experience when I say that
wherever he was, whatever may have been his
apparent preoccupations, in the transaction of
the business of the State there were never any
arrears, there was never any trace of confusion,
there was never any moment of avoidable delay.
Next to these, sir—I am still in the domain of practice and administration—I should put a singular,
perhaps an unrivalled, tact in the management
of men, and a judgment of intuitive shrewdness
as to the best outlet from perplexed and often
baffling situations. He had in its highest and
best development the genius of common-sense.

These rare gifts of practical efficiency were,
during the whole of his Kingship, yoked to the
service of a great ideal. He was animated,
every day of his Sovereignty, by the thought
that he was at once the head and the chief
servant of that vast and complex organism
which we call the British Empire. He recognised
in the fullest degree both the powers and the
limitations of a Constitutional Monarch. Here,
at home, he was, though no politician—as every
one knows—a keen Social Reformer. Already,
as Prince of Wales, he had entered with zeal into
the work of two Royal Commissions—one on the
Housing of the Working Classes, and the other
on the problems connected with the Aged Poor.
His magnificent service to our hospitals, both
before and after his accession, will never be

forgotten. He loved his people at home and over the seas. Their interests were his interests, and their fame was his fame. He had no self apart from them.

I will not touch for more than a moment on more delicate and sacred ground; on his personal charm, the warmth and wealth of his humanity, his unfailing considerateness for all who in any capacity were permitted to work for him. I will only say in this connection that no man in our time has been more justly beloved by his family and his friends, and no ruler in our or in any time has been more sincerely true, more unswervingly loyal, more uniformly kind to his advisers and his servants. By the unsearchable counsels of the Disposer of Events he has been called, suddenly and without warning, to his account. We are still dazed under the blow which has befallen us. It is too soon, as yet, even to attempt to realise its full meaning; but this, at least, we may say at once, and with full assurance, that he has left to his people a memory and an example which they will never forget; a memory of great opportunities greatly employed; and an example which the humblest of his subjects may treasure and strive to follow, of simplicity, courage, self-denial, tenacious devotion, up to the last moment of conscious life, to work, to duty, and to service.

I ask the House to join in the condolences

which we offer to our new Sovereign, the expression of our deepest sympathies with her who for nearly fifty years has shared the joys and sorrows, the cares and responsibilities of the King whom we have lost. Here words fail me. The Queen-Mother, to call her by her new title, is already enthroned in the love of the British people. There is not a heart in the Empire which does not beat with sympathy for her to-day in her suffering and sorrow.

To these, our heartfelt condolences, I ask the House to add its congratulations to His Majesty King George V. on his accession to the throne of his ancestors. Our new Sovereign has served a long apprenticeship to his task. He has personally visited almost every part of his world-wide dominions, and none of us can forget the weighty and impressive summary of our Imperial problems which he delivered on his return from Australia. He has the aid and support of a gracious Consort, born and bred among us. He takes upon his shoulders, at a wholly unexpected call, and at a time of stress and difficulty, as heavy a burden as could fall to the lot of man. Let us, the Commons of this United Kingdom, assure him that it is not only the solemn prayer and the eager hope, but that it is the confident belief of his people, that he will show himself a worthy son and successor of the great King whom we mourn to-day.

XV

ALFRED LYTTELTON

XV

ALFRED LYTTELTON [1]

WE should not, I think, be doing justice to the feelings which are uppermost in many of our hearts if we passed to the business of the day without taking notice of the fresh gap which has been made in our ranks by the untimely death of Mr. Alfred Lyttelton. It is a loss of which I hardly trust myself to speak; for apart from ties of relationship, there had subsisted between us, for thirty-three years, a close friendship and affection which no political differences were ever allowed to loosen or even to invade. Nor can I better describe him than by saying that he perhaps, of all men of this generation, came nearest to the mould and ideal of manhood which every English father would like to see his son aspire to, and if possible to attain. The bounty of nature, enriched and developed, not only by early training, but by constant self-discipline through life, blended in him gifts and graces which, taken alone, are rare, and in such

[1] Speech delivered in the House of Commons, July 7, 1913.

attractive union are rarer still. Body, mind, and character—the school-room, the cricket-field, the Bar, the House of Commons—each made its separate contribution of faculty and of experience to a many-sided and harmonious whole. But what he was he gave; gave with such ease and exuberance that I think it may be said without exaggeration that wherever he moved he seemed to radiate vitality and charm. He was, as we here know, a strenuous fighter. He has left behind him no resentments and no enmities; nothing but a gracious memory of a manly and winning personality; the memory of one who served with an unstinted measure of devotion his generation and his country. He has been snatched away in what we thought was the full tide of a buoyant life, still full of promise and of hope. What more can we say? We can only bow once again before the decrees of the Supreme Wisdom. Those who loved him—and they are many—in all schools of opinion, in all ranks and walks of life, when they think of him will say to themselves:

> This was the happy Warrior; this was He
> That every Man in arms should wish to be.

XVI

EARL KITCHENER

XVI

EARL KITCHENER [1]

I beg to move—

That this House will, to-morrow, resolve itself into a Committee to consider an humble Address to His Majesty, praying that His Majesty will give directions that a monument be erected, at the public charge, to the memory of the late Field-Marshal Earl Kitchener, with an inscription expressing the admiration of this House for his illustrious military career, and its gratitude for his devoted services to the State.

When the House adjourned for the Whitsuntide Recess Lord Kitchener had just received a strong and unmistakable expression of its confidence, and the next day he met in private conference a large number of its Members, including some of his most persistent and, as it then seemed, irreconcilable critics, with the result that he and they parted on terms not only of mutual respect, but of complete understanding. I am glad to remember that, at his last interview with me, he expressed his pleasure at what had happened, and his hope that this was the first

[1] Speech delivered in the House of Commons, June 21, 1916.

step in a relationship of growing confidence and sympathy. When we said farewell, after nearly two years of daily intercourse, which had gone on through all the strain and stress of the war, there was no thought on either side of more than a temporary parting; no foreshadowing of a separation which neither time nor space can bridge. Providence, in its wisdom, was preparing for him sudden release from his burden of care and toil. We who for the moment remain —those of us in particular who shared, as I did, his counsel in the greatest emergencies of our time, with ever-growing intimacy and fulness— can only bow our heads before the Supreme Will, with whom are the issues of life and death.

Lord Kitchener, in whatever environment of circumstances or condition he might have been placed, would have been, as he was always and everywhere, a great and a dominant personality. He was tried in many different ordeals, and he always survived and conquered the test. He began his career in the Royal Engineers without any advantage either of birth or of favour. I remember well, about a year ago, when we were talking one day of the importance of promoting young officers who had distinguished themselves in war, he told me that he himself had been for, I think, twelve years, and remained, a subaltern in that fine and illustrious Corps. He never chafed nor fretted after the fashion of smaller

men. The hour came to him, as it comes to all
who have discernment, faculty, and will, and
from that moment his future was assured. His
name is inseparably associated with that of Lord
Cromer in one of the greatest achievements of
our race and time—the emancipation and re-
generation of Egypt. To his genius we owe the
conquest of the Sudan, and to his organising
initiative the process, which has ever since gone
on, of substituting over a vast, to a large extent
a devastated, area, civilisation for barbarism,
justice for caprice and cruelty, a humane and
equitable rule for a desolating and sterilising
tyranny.

From Egypt he was called, in a great Imperial
emergency, to South Africa, where, in due time,
he brought hostilities to a close, and helped to
lay the foundations of that great and rapidly
consolidating fabric which has welded alienated
races, and given us, in the great conflict of to-
day, a unique example of the service which local
autonomy can render to Imperial strength. The
next stage of his life was given to India, where
he reconstituted and reorganised our Army,
native and British.

Recalled to Egypt, he was displaying the same
gifts in civil administration which he had already
illustrated in the military sphere, when at the
outbreak of the war he obeyed, with the alacrity
of a man who has become the willing servant of

duty, the summons to direct and to recreate our Imperial Forces in the supreme crisis of our national history. He brought to his new task the same sleepless energy, the same resourcefulness, the same masterful personality, which never failed him in any of the fields of action in which he was, during nearly fifty years, called on behalf of his country to play his part. His career has been cut short while still in the exercise and promise of unexhausted powers and possibilities. No one is less fitted than I feel myself at this moment to be, to make an analysis or appraisement of his services to the State. I will only say this, that few men that I have known had less reason to shrink from submitting their lives to

> those pure eyes
> And perfect witness of all-judging Jove.

THE END